HIGHER GROUND

*Coffee Shop Chronicles to Lift Your
Heart and Soul*

Jan Unfried

Higher Ground, Coffee Shop Chronicles to Lift Your Heart and Soul Copyright © 2022 by Jan Unfried. All Rights Reserved.

All rights reserved. No part of this book may be reproduced in any form or by any electronic or mechanical means including information storage and retrieval systems, without permission in writing from the author. The only exception is by a reviewer, who may quote short excerpts in a review.

Cover photograph: Mountains at Lake Tahoe by Jerry Unfried

Follow Common Ground, Solid Ground, and Higher Ground on Facebook @ Jan Unfried's Grounds for Hope

THE HOLY BIBLE, NEW INTERNATIONAL VERSION®, NIV® Copyright © 1973, 1978, 1984, 2011 by Biblica, Inc.™ Used by permission. All rights reserved worldwide.

Jan Unfried
Visit my website at www.janunfried.com

Printed in the United States of America

First Printing: March 2022
J & J Unfried Publishing

ISBN- 979-8-4393-2355-5

Books and Resources by Jan Unfried

Coffee Shop Chronicles Series:

1) *Common Ground, Coffee Shop Chronicles to Warm Your Heart and Soul*

2) *Solid Ground, Coffee Shop Chronicles to Anchor Your Heart and Soul*

3) *Solid Ground Bible Study*

4) *Higher Ground, Coffee Shop Chronicles to Lift Your Heart and Soul*

Jan's Blog: https://www.janunfried.com/blog

Endorsements

Everyone needs real life stories to encourage and build faith in God. Jan Unfried has written some incredible stories from church friends whose lives have been taken to a HIGHER GROUND as a result of their faith and obedience to God. This book will be a valuable addition to your personal devotion time as you sit with a good cup of coffee and read each chapter filled with God's Word and everyday life.

>Pastor Kevin Hardy, Lead Pastor
>Olive Knolls Nazarene Church

I love reading a book by someone who lives out their message with passion and devotion. Jan is just such a person. Her love for Jesus is undeniable. Her hunger to see wandering sheep come home to the Good Shepherd is contagious. Her wisdom about faith sharing is a gift to the church and the world. I pray that this book will inspire your heart, impact your life, and open your mouth to share the world-changing good news of Jesus.

>Rev. Dr. Kevin G. Harney
>Founder of Organic Outreach International (organicoutreach.org)
>Author of *Organic Outreach Trilogy* and *Organic Disciples*
>Lead Pastor of Shoreline Church in Monterey, Ca.

Jesus spoke in parables to meet his listeners where they were at with eternal truths. Jan Unfried uses relatable modern-day, real-life stories of people of faith to help illustrate the timeless truths of scripture. Her latest book, HIGHER GROUND, will inspire, challenge, and transform the way you perceive your daily experiences—to look beyond the mundane to the ordained encounters where God is at work in your life.

    Pastor Brent Kall, Discipleship and Small Groups Pastor
    Olive Knolls Nazarene Church

Acknowledgements

Writing *Higher Ground* has certainly been more of a challenge than the first two books! I expected to have it ready by Fall of 2020, but the coronavirus interrupted those plans. Some of you have waited quite a while to see your story finally in print!

My heart is full of thanks to all of those who were willing to share your stories. We did it through Zoom meetings, phone calls, sitting six feet apart in person, and with masks. More than ever, I needed the encouragement that came from your testimonies. I am excited that others will now be able to receive that same inspiration. There would not be a *Coffee Shop Chronicles 3* without you.

Thank you to my husband, Jerry, for spending tireless hours taking photographs, editing pictures and text, saving receipts, traveling the countryside, and listening to me process my thoughts. You are such a blessing in my life.

Patti King and Terie Storar, my friends and editors, thank you for making time to read and edit my stories. Your support and encouragement to me through my book projects has been above and beyond friendship. You have certainly earned a few extra jewels in your crown, as far as I'm concerned.

Last, but not least, I am so grateful for Jesus, who continued to lift me up through the crazy times of the pandemic and to assure me of His perfect timing for the completion of *Higher Ground*.

Table of Contents

Introduction 1

Adventures on Higher Ground 5

Chapter 1 The Alps of the Bible 6
Chapter 2 Against All Hope 14
Chapter 3 The Apple (Strudel) of Temptation 23
Chapter 4 View from the Top 32
Chapter 5 Joy?...Now?...How? 40
Chapter 6 Don't Fight the Flight 49
Chapter 7 A Heavenly Planting 57
Chapter 8 The Lord's Timing 65
Chapter 9 The Loft 74
Chapter 10 Give Me the Hill Country 81

Journeys to Higher Ground 89

Chapter 11 The Shelter of the Most High 90
Chapter 12 God is for You 99
Chapter 13 God's Hand 108
Chapter 14 Where and How? 115
Chapter 15 The Sweet Taste of Joy 122
Chapter 16 A Work in Progress 131
Chapter 17 From Mourning to Dancing 139
Chapter 18 One in a Million 149
Chapter 19 When I am Weak 158
Chapter 20 It's Yours 167

Choosing Higher Ground **176**
   Chapter 21 Hindsight is 2020 ....*177*
   Chapter 22 Rise *187*
   Chapter 23 Shoe Grace *196*
   Chapter 24 The Bride of the Lamb *203*
   Chapter 25 Train Up a Child *210*
   Chapter 26 Seeing the God Who Sees *220*
   Chapter 27 Lord, Give Me Strength *228*
   Chapter 28 Lost and Found *236*
   Chapter 29 Scale the Wall *243*
   Chapter 30 God Goes Before You *251*

INTRODUCTION

There is a familiar hymn called "Higher Ground" that I grew up singing in church. The chorus rings out with these words:

> My heart has no desire to stay
> Where doubts arise and fears dismay.
> Tho' some may dwell where these abound,
> My prayer, my aim, is higher ground.
> Johnson Oatman, Jr.[1]

Higher Ground, Coffee Shop Chronicles to Lift Your Heart and Soul, will share how God has lifted people above their circumstances to a higher place. Let me first explain what "higher ground" is NOT. It is NOT placing someone on a pedestal. Face it! Every human will eventually fall off. It is NOT a holier-than-thou attitude that brags, "Look at me, I'm above it all." Finally, it is NOT putting our head in the clouds and ignoring reality. "Higher ground" IS a recognition that the "ground" we rejoice over is not our circumstances. Our joy comes from delighting in the Lord, regardless of circumstances, which enables us to live **above** them. ***Higher Ground*** is a deep recognition that His ways are higher than my ways (see Isaiah 55:8-9).

Make no mistake, getting to higher ground takes work! When we want to get to the top of a mountain, we must plan the trip, prepare the proper equipment and supplies, train our muscles, and be ready for the unexpected. Spiritually, we have to do the same. We must be disciplined to seek God's map, His Word, so that we can then

---

[1] Oatman, Jr., Johnson. "Higher Ground." *Worship in Song.* Lillenas Publishing Co., 1972.

maintain the connection with God that reminds us of who He is and who we are in Him. We must put on the proper spiritual armor (see Ephesians 6:10-18) so that we can be prepared for the daily grind as well as the challenging hills. We must flex our prayer muscles on a regular basis so that we feel His presence as we navigate through each day.

None of this guarantees that life will be like floating on a cloud, nor does it mean ignoring our real and concrete issues. Again, that is NOT the higher ground this book describes. These stories are of real people, going through real trials, who experience real victory in Jesus! They seek a deep walk with God, wanting to know Him, and the power of His resurrection, while experiencing the fellowship of His sufferings (see Philippians 3:10).

With this being the third book in the *Coffee Shop Chronicles*, let's consider how coffee grown at higher elevations affects the taste of coffee. Higher elevations produce hard, dense beans that are greatly sought after. The beans at these heights are of a greater quality than beans that grow in lower elevations because they have a higher concentration of sugar. The cool temperatures cause the beans to mature more slowly, providing time for complex sugars to develop. These sugars create amazing taste-notes that are not seen in the beans at lower elevations. The other major difference is in the watershed. Better drainage on the mountainside leads to less water in the beans, allowing for greater concentration of these same flavors.

Growing coffee at higher elevations is harder on the coffee farmer. Greater care must be taken to ensure the coffee plants flourish. Fewer plants survive, making the work twice as hard to produce the volume that is needed during harvest. The final result, however, is always worth it to the coffee connoisseur. It is a merited task to check the label that indicates the elevation at which the coffee was grown.

As you read these stories, I hope that you will continually check your own elevation. Have you been doing the work of aiming for higher ground? It is not a pie-in-the-sky place to land. It is the on-going work of the Holy Spirit in our lives that enables us to mature slowly and meaningfully, developing the rich flavors of love and grace that keep our lives from becoming bogged down in the watershed of tough circumstances.

Don't be discouraged! God will be with you every step of the way! Most of us do not want to "stay where doubts arise and fears dismay." Stay grounded in God and His word, keep connected with others who can encourage and support you in prayer along the way, and allow God's power in these stories to lift you to *Higher Ground*.

FOR YOUR INFORMATION:

There are some things set up in each chapter of this book to help you get the most out of *Higher Ground, Coffee Shop Chronicles to Lift Your Heart and Soul.* Of course, you can absorb each chapter as a read-through only. If you want to go deeper and/or use it as a daily devotional, each chapter is summarized in a section called "**Summing it Up.**" There are verses that support these key points in a segment called "**Highlights from God's Word**." You are also given an opportunity to journal your thoughts about the chapter content, summary points, or scriptures on a page called "**Memos of Mountain-top Moments.**" No matter how you choose to go through the book, I hope that your faith will be lifted to new heights.

Finally, you will find that many of the chronicles make reference to Olive Knolls Church. Olive Knolls Church of the Nazarene is in Bakersfield, California. It is my home church, and, though not exclusively, I have interviewed a lot of people from my church family. Our lead pastor, Rev. Darren Reed, from my other two books moved to Denver, CO, in 2020. Our new pastor is Rev. Kevin Hardy. Rather than explaining this in each separate chapter, the church may be referred to interchangeably as Olive Knolls, Olive Knolls Church, or Olive Knolls Nazarene Church. Occasionally I will refer to the pastor as Pastor Kevin. I know you all have a church body that has amazing stories like the ones you will read here. I urge you to take a friend or two to coffee and share your miracles with each other. I pray you will be encouraged and uplifted.

Jan

JAN UNFRIED'S
Grounds FOR Hope
ROM 15:13

Adventures on Higher Ground

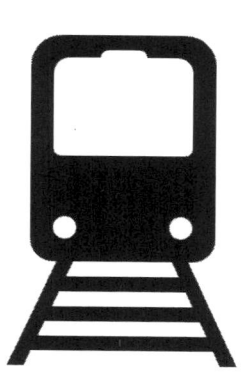

Chapter 1
THE ALPS OF THE BIBLE

Praise be to the God and Father of our Lord Jesus Christ, who has blessed us in the heavenly realms with every spiritual blessing in Christ. Ephesians 1:3

A couple of years ago, our pastor at Olive Knolls was preaching a sermon series on the book of Ephesians. He commented that the book of Ephesians is known as the "Alps of the Scripture." I immediately thought of the book I was working on, *Higher Ground*, and I determined to look into Ephesians in depth.

Before we get into the lessons in Ephesians, let me first say that I love the mountains. We camped in the California peaks with our boys every summer. Our favorite spot was nestled in the campgrounds of Hume Lake in the Sierra Nevada Mountain range. The fresh air and the smell and sound of pine trees rustling in the breeze always filled my soul.

As a teen, I had the opportunity to visit Switzerland and made a train trek by cog railway to the beautiful resort village of Zermatt to view the Matterhorn. The town was quaint, with shops lining its main streets. The center, or hub, of the town, was graced by the train station and the Parish church of Saint Mauritius. The simple architecture and white steeple made a beautiful contrast against the purple hills. It was not uncommon throughout the day to see sheep and goat herders cross in front of us, guiding their livestock toward their next destination. It was an idyllic town, everything being within a walk of thirty-minutes or less.

The awe-inspiring view of the mountain overlooking the village produced chills down my spine. There was snow, in spite of the summer temperatures in the valley, but it was the magnificence and splendor of the peak that incited the wonder I felt. This peak, rising 14,692 feet in elevation serves as the natural border between Switzerland and Italy. Its northern face was not successfully climbed until 1931, after several failed attempts of man versus nature.

God's creative beauty and majesty cannot be outdone. How He must have delighted in creating the world. As he took His time crafting the oceans, the streams, the rivers, the deserts, the mountains, and the valleys, He must have been thinking of those He would create in His likeness. He knew we would love and appreciate Him even more as we enjoyed His artistry prepared for us. He knew His invisible qualities—His power and divine nature—would be clearly seen in His creation.

My love for the mountains and the Alps probably explains why my favorite musical and movie is *The Sound of Music.* People seem to either agree wholeheartedly with my opinion, or they immediately turn their nose up at the thought of the Von Trapp family hiking through the hills singing "Doe a Deer." Yet, as the musical opens on the beautiful Alpine slopes, and Maria, the main character, sings "The hills are alive with the sound of music," it is just one more reminder that creation truly does rejoice and sing of the glory of God.

In researching the concept of the Alps of scripture found in Ephesians, I found that the term "heavenly realms" occurs several times throughout the six short chapters of this New Testament book. The first of these references is, "Praise be to the God and

Father of our Lord Jesus Christ, who has blessed us in the heavenly realms with every spiritual blessing in Christ" (Ephesians 1:3). We have every blessing that comes from above, right here, right now. I'd say that is pretty lofty stuff!

Unfortunately, we do not always live as if we believe that we are blessed and have at our fingertips the same access to the kingdom as Jesus does. The following is a list of a few blessings that He offers to us throughout Ephesians. We are:

- Chosen
- Holy & Blameless
- Loved
- Adopted
- Accepted
- Redeemed
- Forgiven
- Abounding in Grace
- An Heir
- Full of Hope
- Given access to His power

I don't know about you, but that list makes me want to sing from the mountain tops. I actually think I hear a few of you yodeling!

The next look at the phrase "heavenly realms" can be found in Ephesians 2:6: "And God raised us up with Christ and seated us with him in the heavenly realms in Christ Jesus." Again, all I can say is, "Wow!" Being seated with Christ in Heaven is giving us **EVERYTHING**, even though we **DON'T DESERVE IT**! It's called grace. We cannot do anything to earn it. He gives it to us freely when we receive and trust in Him for our salvation. The only reaction, other than "Wow!" is to respond with good works which God prepared in advance for us to do (See Ephesians 2:10).

Each morning as we get out of bed, we should be asking God, "How can I serve You through my deeds and actions today?" Can you imagine the **higher ground** we would be standing on if every Christian sincerely lived the way Christ intended for us to live?

The next reference to "heavenly realms" comes from Ephesians 3:10-11, which states, "His intent was that now, through the church, the manifold wisdom of God should be made known to the rulers and authorities in the heavenly realms, according to his eternal purpose which he accomplished in Christ Jesus our Lord."

What does this mean for us? We are the vessel, the church, through which the rest of the universe sees the wisdom of God. The world should be able to get a glimpse of Christ's eternal purpose when it sees our love for Him and for each other. He came to reconcile and unite all mankind to God. Believers in Jesus have the privilege and honor to be the conduit of His reconciliation to the world.

Oh, if we would only get on board the cog railway to this height. The church should be displaying love and unity, truth and grace, that is so attractive and inviting that all those around us desire that same relationship and peace in Christ. We have a huge responsibility to serve and build Christ's kingdom in this way. We can either fuel the fire of disunity (which can so easily get out of control), or we can stoke the flames of the Holy Spirit of God which has the power to strongly unite.

The final reference of "heavenly realms" I found in this letter from the apostle Paul is in Ephesians 6:12. "For our struggle is not against flesh and blood, but against the rulers, against the authorities, against the powers of this dark world and against the spiritual forces of evil in the heavenly realms."

If we can grasp this one thing, we will really understand our blessings in Christ. We struggle so much trying to fight the earthly battles: "this person said this or that..." "this group thinks wrongly," and so on. We look at our human disagreements as the problem, and we spin our wheels trying to solve spiritual battles with mere human resources.

No wonder we get tired and discouraged. Our focus should not be in addressing our opposition, but in getting dressed for the proper battle! By putting on the full armor of God, we can face down the enemy of this age. Sometimes we make easy prey for Satan when we don't recognize that he is trying to devour us. We are not spiritually prepared! We must understand and claim that He who is in us is greater than He who is in the world (see 1 John 4:4). We have everything we need to live victoriously!

We all have different battles that we are facing today. Christ wants you to go forward with His power and live in the benefits of His kingdom, NOW. We have the power of prayer. We have the resources to rise above our circumstances and live on **higher ground**. The following chapters will give you some real-life examples of how this has been done in modern times, in His kingdom here on Earth. I am excited for you to share in these experiences. Let's trek into the Alps together!

Summing it Up:

- God's invisible qualities—His power and divine nature—can be clearly seen in His creation.
- Creation truly does rejoice and sing of the glory of God.
- We are blessed with every spiritual blessing that is in Christ Jesus, but we do not always live as if we believe that we are blessed and have at our fingertips the same access to the kingdom as Jesus does.
- Being seated with Christ in Heaven is giving us EVERYTHING, even though we DON'T DESERVE IT! It's called grace.
- The only reaction, other than "Wow!" is to respond with good works which God prepared in advance for us to do.
- Jesus came to reconcile and unite all mankind to God, and we have the privilege and honor to be the conduit for this reconciliation.
- We can either fuel the fire of disunity (which can so easily get out of control), or we can stoke the flames of the fire of the Spirit of God which has the power to strongly unite.
- We look at our human disagreements as the problem, and we spin our wheels trying to solve spiritual battles

with mere human resources instead of living victoriously.
- Our focus should not be in addressing our opposition, but in getting dressed for the proper battle!

☀ Highlights from God's Word:
- Romans 1:20
- Psalm 96:11-12
- Ephesians 1:3
- Ephesians 2:6
- Ephesians 2:10
- Ephesians 3:10-11
- 2 Timothy 1:6-7
- Ephesians 6:12; 1 John 4:4
- Ephesians 6:13-18

Memos of Mountaintop Moments

Chapter 2
AGAINST ALL ODDS

Against all hope, Abraham in hope believed and so became the father of many nations, just as it had been said to him, "So shall your offspring be." Romans 4:18

The excitement was mounting! Randy and Elaine were on a three-week European tour. One of their goals for the trip was to celebrate their 50th wedding anniversary by renewing their commitment to each other. Because they were a part of a tour group, the timing had to be perfect. Brendan, their guide, was getting into the excitement of helping them plan this special occasion. Several times along the way, he let them know that the location was great, but the schedule didn't leave sufficient time for their ceremony. Brendan had never had a couple ask for anything like this in his years of leading tourists through Europe, but he was confident he would know when everything was just right.

Toward the end of the trip, Brendan was taking the group 7,000 feet up to Mount Pilatus, a massif in Central Switzerland that overlooks Lake Lucerne and the surrounding city. He made the announcement! This was it!

Elaine had purchased an outfit to wear for the occasion. Both Randy and Elaine had prepared the words they wanted to say to renew the covenant they had made between themselves and God fifty years ago. Their fellow tourists, many of whom had become friends as they had spent long days together trekking through new and exciting places of awesome wonder, were anticipating their participation as "witnesses" to this grand event.

As they were transported to **higher ground** via cable cars, Elaine quickly realized that her new outfit would not be visible in any of the pictures that were to be taken. It was a "mild" seventeen degrees at the peak of their destination. She never took off her "ushanka" (a Russian winter hat) or her borrowed, thigh-length, puffy jacket. In spite of the cold, while overlooking a spectacular view, Randy and Elaine shared the warmth of the love that God had built between them.

At one time, it had been against all hope that this marriage would have lasted even a few years, much less fifty! But God extends His hope to us. He promises abundant life, and then, when the world is ready to give up and throw in the towel, He comes through. The Bible provides story after story of God working against hopelessness:
- No one would have expected Abraham and Sarah to have a child in their old age.
- It seemed impossible that the Israelites could escape from Pharaoh's oppression.
- It was beyond anyone's hope or imagination that Jesus would conquer death and live again!
- The persecuted Christians certainly wouldn't have put their hope in the conversion of Saul of Tarsus!
- No one would have imagined Jews and Gentiles worshiping the one true God together.

God still works today beyond our hopes and expectations. For the Mosley's it was beyond their scope of thought that they would be telling their story to a Hindu teen and her mother. When the young lady asked Elaine what they meant by making a "covenant with God," Elaine got permission from the girl's parents, a Singapore couple who was in their travel group. She simply explained how a relationship with Jesus had given them access to God. They could communicate directly to God through prayer as they made the promise to Him and to each other that they would stay together no matter what happened. With God as part of their covenant, they knew He would help them with their vows. It was a commitment that would be tested through time.

Randy and Elaine will tell you that it was against all odds that they passed the longevity test of their relationship. They were told by family and friends that their marriage wouldn't last. They were only eighteen years of age when they entered married "bliss," which was way too young to be able to weather the ups and downs of life together. Randy's immediate entry into the Marine Corps required uprooting their home ties. There were also lengthy stints of time when Randy was overseas, and they were separated from each other. Without the conveniences of the Internet and cell service, they were lucky to have a three-minute phone conversation a couple of times a year. As Elaine put it, the call was just long enough to make her start crying.

Once Randy was finished with his military obligations, he got a job with the Tulare County Sherriff's Department. Elaine recalled the interview the department had with her, as part of the vetting process for hiring her husband. In no uncertain terms, they wanted to make sure she was aware that those who chose this line of work were subject to the nationwide statistic of having the highest percentage of divorce rate. To top it off, Randy was offered a station in Pixley, a little nondescript Central California Valley town with a population of less than 3,000. One look at the town had Elaine declaring she would never live there!

Nevertheless, Randy accepted the job, and they ended up calling Pixley their home for the next decade or so. Elaine settled into a job with the school district as a teacher's aide. The friendships they formed in this little community were part of the way God worked in and through their marriage trials in the next few years. As Elaine said, "God put people in place long before we knew we needed them."

Elaine was privileged to work with two teachers who were both wonderful godly people! Her principal, a no-nonsense type of guy, was a man of faith who gave wise guidance during a critical time. A couple of neighborhood ladies called on them relentlessly, inviting them to their church. The Mosley's began attending the United Brethren Church in Pixley. Former Baptists, they had never heard of this denomination, but they found the small congregation to be loving and warm. They immersed themselves in service to the church and community. Things looked calm on the surface, but underneath, at home, a storm was beginning to brew.

Randy worked the night-shifts. He enjoyed the hours, though they were typically filled with activity and high stress. When he and his buddies got off at 7:00 AM, it was like everyone else's 5:00 PM. In need of decompressing after their shift, Randy and his co-workers would grab a beer and hang out at a local park for a few hours to debrief and unwind. By the time Randy got home to try to catch some sleep before his next shift, Elaine and the girls were off to school. Things went along for a while without incident, but Elaine was beginning to miss communicating with Randy and working together as a team to build their home.

Over time, when Elaine would "gently" remind Randy of his short-comings, she would be met with a defensive attitude. The gentleness would often turn into a shouting match, ending with nothing resolved. Elaine wanted Randy to stop drinking. Randy knew it was just a social outlet for himself after a long night of work. They couldn't see eye-to-eye, and they were not meeting heart-to-heart over anything!

What Elaine wanted most was to stay married, but she wanted a good marriage, not a splintered one. She began to lie in bed at night trying to figure out how she and the girls could survive on her meager salary alone. The numbers did not add up, but one day she packed her things. She let Randy know she was leaving with the car (he could have the truck), and she was taking the girls with her.

A few nights later, around 1:00 AM, Elaine received a phone call from the pastor. Randy was in the pastor's living room, and the pastor wanted to know if she would come over to talk. Elaine's hackles raised. She was not about to go over there to hear them tell her she needed to stop being a nagging wife. She didn't want to be told she should learn to accept things as they were. When she finally quieted her mind and spirit enough to hear what was happening on the other end of the phone, she dropped her defenses and listened. Randy was broken and ready to apologize and make changes.

Against all hope, the Mosley's relationship was reconciled, and they rededicated their lives and their marriage to God. They began attending Olive Knolls Church in Bakersfield, and they renewed their wedding vows on their 25th anniversary. They began to attend a small group, and became intimately involved with other couples who were like-minded in things of the Lord. They are forever grateful for the miracle God worked in their lives.

We can learn some crucial lessons through the Mosley's lives. First, our Covenant God is faithful to keep His promises to us. He knows that covenant relationships take sacrifice, love, and work. He exemplified this throughout Biblical history and in the life of His Son, Jesus Christ. When we covenant with Him in our marriage, our work, and our families, we are not entering a world without storms. We are venturing into places where we can learn, grow, and allow God to smooth out our rough edges. We can do it because God is guiding us through it. Lori Margo, author and speaker, says, "Life is hard, AND God is incredible." We can embrace the "AND" because He promises to never leave us alone!

Second, God places people in our lives that He knows we need, even before we are aware of how much we need them. Some of those people are assumed mentors, like our pastors or parents. Others are surprises! They are the quiet influencers who have a relationship with the Covenant God, and are praying for us behind the scenes. They are the ones who watch and listen for the Holy Spirit to nudge them to take action at just the right time. They rely on Yahweh, the covenant name of God, which indicates His strength, as well as His sovereignty and goodness. They are there to help us pray through our difficulties. They help us bridge the gap between our desperation and God's will for our lives.

Finally, God uses our struggles and pain for His good. Randy and Elaine have been able to help couples who are going through marriage difficulties. They have the "credentials" because they have been through the fire and have come out refined like silver. Their lives are examples to all of us that God is in the business of redemption and reconciliation. God can turn all of our trials into miracles of His grace! Against all hope, when there seems to be no human possibility or solution, God delivers!

What do you need to place your faith in God for today? Do you have an impossible marriage? Is your son or daughter too far gone for you to see them coming back? Have you made decisions that seem to have irreversible destructive consequences? Has a traumatic event or past left you feeling dead inside? Abraham, in hope, believed (see Romans 4:18). The Mosley's, in hope, believed, though their marriage was as good as dead. You can place your hope in God for your circumstance as well.

Nothing is too difficult for God! Can you sense it? He created the magnificent scenic mountain scape at the top of the Swiss Ural Alps. He created the beautiful union between husband and wife. God always works with our good in mind. You don't need to climb to an elevation of 7,000 feet to experience the height of God's love! He will bring you hope right where you are!

Summing it Up:

- God extends His hope to us. He promises abundant life, and then, when the world is ready to give up and throw in the towel, He comes through.
- Our Covenant God is faithful to keep His promises to us. He knows that covenant relationships take sacrifice, love, and work. He promises to never leave us alone!
- God places people in our lives that He knows we need, even before we are aware of how much we need them.
- God can turn all of our trials into miracles of His grace! Against all hope, when there seems to be no human possibility or solution, God delivers!

☀ Highlights from God's Word:
- Romans 4:18-21
- 1 Thessalonians 5:23-24, Deuteronomy 31:8
- Matthew 6:8
- Luke 1:37

Memos of Mountaintop Moments

Chapter 3
THE APPLE (STRUDEL) OF TEMPTATION

When the woman saw that the fruit of the tree was good for food and pleasing to the eye, and also desirable for gaining wisdom, she took some and ate it. Genesis 3:6a

They spent a night lost in the Swiss Alps. Some called it luck that they made it to safety the next day without suffering hypothermia. Some gave credit to the foehn /fən, fān/, a dry, warm, down-slope wind that occurs in the lee of a mountain range. Still others gave credit to the experienced hikers in the group.

If you ask the five that were involved, they would all agree on two things. One, it was the apple strudel that got them into trouble to begin with. Second, it was the provision and protection of God that saved them from certain peril.

Although their adventure occurred twenty years ago, Carol retold it as if it were yesterday. She and her then sixty-nine-year-old mom had traveled to Switzerland. Mixing business with pleasure, they attached some vacation plans at the tail end of their trip. As they visited with friends, Max and Gina, and their three kids, they made plans to travel to the peak of Mount Pilatus. Gina and her older daughter were going to stay in town and do some shopping.

The rest of the crew took the gondola ride up the mountainside to the 6,982-foot peak.

Over lunch, plans were made to hike down the "hill." Max, a dual US/Swiss citizen, had completed the trail multiple times, and had full confidence they could all successfully traverse the downward route. They were supposed to meet Gina at a café for some of the best apple strudel in Switzerland. The pastry party was a non-negotiable, so Max began to look for the best way to get to their rendezvous point.

The trail markers at the top of the hill pointed in two different directions. The first arrow was the path he was familiar with, but the second arrow clearly indicated the trek to their much-anticipated treat. The group of five, ranging from age twelve to sixty-nine, began their journey around 2:30 PM. They were clad in "Pick & Save" sweatshirts and borrowed tennis shoes. They carried a couple of lemon bars and a water bottle between them, and they held a mutual enthusiasm for an epic adventure.

The chosen "treat" trail proved difficult to follow due to the fall foliage. The path had also been compromised by the hooves of cattle that had been herded to lower ground before the winter months began in full. They found out later that the trail was mismarked, and after their adventure the sign was removed permanently from the top of the mountain. It wasn't long before they realized that the marked way was non-existent. Instead of turning around and retracing their steps, the group decided that they would be able to find their way by following the river below them.

We often find ourselves heading in a compromising direction in life. The best course of action would be to repent (turn around), and get to **higher ground** so that we can get a safer perspective. Instead, we tend to trudge forward, willing ourselves to believe that it will get better soon. God provides a way out (see 1 Corinthians 10:12-13). We just need to heed His voice.

As they made their way down into the river's ravine, the way became more and more precarious. They scooted along on their backsides, continuing to traverse downward, the logical direction of their goal. The sunlit terrain quickly became shadowed and then completely darkened by the fading daylight and the tall mountains. The two younger ones were sent ahead to scout the best route for the wearying group of adults. Fourteen-year-old Andrew got too far ahead of himself, and was soon separated from his sister and the rest of the gang.

It was becoming apparent that they should not continue, as night had come upon them. There were too many dangerous slopes and precipices to maneuver in the impending dark. As they continued to call out for Andrew, the four who were still together decided to find a safe spot for the night. Andrew was not too far away, but he could not hear their calls over the flowing river and nearby waterfall.

Twelve-year-old Susan was the one that spotted a ledge that seemed flat and safe for the night. At the end of the ledge stood a tree, secure in the ground. At this point Carol remembers ramping up her prayers. She was praying for Andrew's safety, for Max's wisdom, and for all of them to be rescued. The night was quickly growing colder and there was a threat of a possible storm arriving soon.

They shared one of the lemon bars and some water, and hunkered down for a long night. Max had them line up like centipedes, each one with their legs wrapped around the person in front of them. Carol was in the front of the line with her legs wrapped around the tree. Intertwined in this fashion made it less likely they would roll off the cliff if, and when, they fell asleep. The tree offered them a source of stability and strength, an anchor in the rock.

God is our anchor during our difficult times. He provides stability when we are on unsure ground. It might be a sudden loss, a broken relationship, or a life-changing decision you must make. No matter what, God is the stable source we can rely on. He wants us to lean into Him and wrap our arms around Him. He wants us to feel the safety-net of His consistent and loving presence in our lives. He gives us amazing hope (see Hebrews 6:19).

As the group began to sing hymns and Christian choruses to keep their spirits lifted and their minds focused on the positive, Carol continued to pray. God taught her a couple of important lessons that night about prayer. First, she believed that the Holy Spirit was urging her to stay away from negative thoughts and "what-if" scenarios. She kept her mind engaged in good and praiseworthy thoughts. She focused on solutions and actions. Besides singing, the group of four would periodically move their arms in circles to keep their body heat up and to maintain circulation flow. They told stories and shared good memories. They kept the presence of God in the forefront of all their thoughts.

It's so easy to run down the rabbit trail of negativity when we are facing a problem. Not only are we to ask for help, but we are to rejoice, and dwell on whatever is true, noble, right, pure, lovely, and admirable (see Philippians 4:4-9). There are always fearful possibilities to dwell on, but God wants us to be joyful and fearless in the face of these because He has promised to be near us.

The other lesson Carol remembers came through a question from God that was almost audible, asking her, "What do you want me to do?" He was asking her to pray specifically. Up until now her prayers had been broad sweeping prayers: "Lord save us." She now began to pray, "Lord, protect Andrew. Stave off the rain, and somehow put a pocket of warmth around us."

Even when we are in a perilous situation, we often make our prayers general and imprecise. God asks us, as He asked the blind man on the road from Jericho, "What do you want me to do for you?" (see Mark 10:51). Wasn't it obvious this man wanted his sight? Wasn't it obvious that Carol and her companions wanted to be saved through the night? Jesus wants us to ask specifically, and in His name, so that through the faith of our specific requests, we will know that it was God who answered, beyond a shadow of a doubt.

For this motley crew, it was not luck as some surmised, but the hand of God who answered specific prayer! The Lord sent the foehn. This wind shadowed the rain that had fallen on the windward slopes of the mountain, and significantly increased the temperature that evening. It also kept the precipitation away from their location. Carol and her mom, Lauraine, can remember feeling pockets of warmth surrounding them intermittently throughout the bone-cold chill of the night.

At the light of day, they could see how perilous their position had really been. They rejoiced that they had made it through the harrowing night, and they were ready to figure out their next steps. Again, they scooted along a ridge on their bottoms to avoid plummeting into a five-foot pool of ice-cold water below. Muscles sore and shaky from the ordeal, they pushed their bodies to keep moving. After a failed attempt in one direction, which ended in a sheer drop-off, Max finally spotted a trail.

They made their way to the unmaintained path. They had to traverse fallen logs, going over one and under two more. The weary group had to literally work together to pull Lauraine through the last of the under-log tunnels. To their elation, they were soon spotted by a Swiss-native hiker who was actually out looking for this reported lost group of Americans. His name was Joseph. Carol recalls thinking that he was an angel sent to them to finish the rescue effort.

Joseph led them to the café at the bottom of the hill that had been their original destination. The girls got a warm drink and something to eat. Joseph and Max went back out to look for Andrew. Carol and Lauraine suddenly noticed that everyone in the café seemed to be staring and pointing at these "celebrities." Their pictures and story had been all over the news since the night before when Gina had reported them missing. The local residents were seeing a miracle before their eyes. The rescue team had departed that morning with body bags, fully expecting to find that the trekkers had not survived the freezing, wet night. The ladies were soon surrounded by news stations and newspaper reporters.

Meanwhile, Andrew had used his scouting skills to surround himself through the night with a circle of sticks staked deeply into the ground to keep himself from falling downhill and over a precipice. He had realized that it was best to not try to follow the voices of his family and friends once it had become dark. In the morning, he continued to traverse upward. He felt if he could find the railroad track of the cogwheel rail, he might get to safety. Sure enough, an engineer spotted him, stopped to allow him to board the train, and radioed that he would be delivered to a nearby station at 3:00 PM. Close to twenty-four hours later, the entire group of five, joined by Gina, reunited with enormous relief, extreme exhaustion, and exuberant joy.

They never did get to taste the ill-advised strudel. Instead, a waitress at the restaurant where they awaited Matthew's arrival brought them a steaming bowl of the best stew they had ever tasted. It brought them warmth and nourishment that they so needed. Let me be clear, I do not have anything against apple strudel, but we often think we "want" the strudel of life. We are tempted, like Eve in the garden, to descend a perilous path to receive it. God teaches us in His gentle and caring way that what we really "need" is to look for the path on **higher ground**, and to partake of His hearty and nourishing "meat and vegetables." He will meet our true needs!

Summing it Up:

- God provides a way out of our temptations and treacherous paths. We just need to heed His voice.
- It's so easy to run down the rabbit trail of negativity when we are facing a problem, but God wants us to be joyful and fearless in the face of these adversities because He has promised to be near us.

- Jesus wants us to ask specifically, and in His name. Then we will know beyond a shadow of a doubt that it was God who answered our specific requests.
- No matter what, God is the stable source we can rely on. He wants us to lean into Him and wrap our arms around Him. He wants us to feel the safety-net of His consistent and loving presence in our lives. He gives us amazing hope
- We often think we "want" the strudel of life. We are tempted to descend a perilous path to receive it. God teaches us in His gentle and caring way that what we really "need" is to look for the path on **higher** ground, and to partake of His hearty and nourishing "meat and vegetables." He will meet our true needs!

☼ Highlights from God's Word:
- 1 Corinthians 10:12-13
- Philippians 4:4-9
- Mark 10:46-52, John 16:23-24
- Hebrews 6:17-20
- Genesis 3: 1-7; Philippians 4:19

Memos of Mountaintop Moments

Chapter 4
VIEW FROM THE TOP

Blessed is the man who perseveres under trial, because when he has stood the test, he will receive the crown of life that God has promised to those who love him. James 1:12

A thought occurred to me the other day. In order to gain a view from the top, we need to dive down first. Until we dive into our issues, we feel stuck, even a little paralyzed. We are unable to move up, down, or through the day. This looks and sounds like depression, and it can take on various intensities. I experienced something like this when I was a young mom of three active boys. I was most likely in denial because I didn't want to appear weak to anyone. Time and wisdom have shown me that depression is not a sign of weakness.

Unfortunately, mental illnesses, such as bipolar disorders or depression, are often misunderstood in the world, especially in the Christian community. People may say things that are based on misconceptions. They may feel like depression isn't real, that it's caused because of sin, or because you do not have enough faith. Depression is as real as a physical illness. We wouldn't judge someone for seeking medical help for an ailment, yet it may be just as appropriate for those experiencing depression to seek professional help. The truth is that God cares deeply about our lives. He will never cut Himself off from us. His love does not depend on us. He may even use depression or other trials to bring about good.

In my particular case, my husband had gone through a couple of job changes for a variety of reasons. After being burned in the business world a few times, he decided he would go back to school to get his teaching credential. We had come close to declaring bankruptcy. For a period of a couple of years, he would have to hold a low-paying, part-time evening job while he attended classes and observed in classrooms during the day. I was going to have to leave my teaching position at Olive Knolls Christian School to work in public education so that we would receive a little extra pay and benefits. None of this was in my scheduled plan of life events.

Without even realizing it, I had begun to feel lost, alone, and overwhelmed. I was weary of us trying to figure out how each month's bills were going to be paid. Two years, though a short time period in the grand scheme of things, seemed like forever. I had enjoyed working at a private Christian school where I could openly teach about Jesus. It was a place of familiarity and comfort, and my three boys were able to attend the same school with me every day. As my despair began to grow, I kept pushing it down.

That fall we were at a family gathering for Thanksgiving. Our after-turkey conversations turned to the Lord and His faithfulness. My mother-in-law has always had a wonderful connection with God and has been a faithful prayer warrior for our families through the years. My hopelessness may have been quite obvious, even though I was sure I was hiding my emotions well, but I believe the Holy Spirit impressed on her that I needed a touch from God. When she asked me how I was doing, the well of tears began to flow. That's not too unusual for me, since I believe I must have the gift of tears, but this became a heartfelt release of my inner conflict.

As she often did, my mother-in-law pulled a small vial of anointing oil from her purse. You might feel a little "weirded out" about this, so let me put you at ease. This was such an organic and authentic way that she prayed and cared for others. She had learned from God's Word that healing came from laying hands on others and praying for them, anointing their heads with oil.

We typically had the person who was being prayed for sit in a chair in the middle of the room so that everyone could gather around them. I was surrounded by adults and little ones (who loved to be a part, even when they probably didn't understand it all). The family's prayers and understanding brought Heaven down into that living room that day.

There was an immediate and miraculous lifting of my depression, a depression that I had not even recognized that I was experiencing. It was like a fog lifted from my brain and allowed me to see that there was a sun shining out there. Somehow, God gave me the insight and foresight that He was in control and that everything was going to be okay. I am so grateful that my plight was temporary. I know it doesn't always happen in such a dramatic fashion. It has nothing to do with a lack of or an extra portion of faith. God, in His sovereignty, chose to heal my spirit in that particular way on that particular day.

The next two years are a bit of a blur in my memory. I just know we made it. My focus turned from my hopelessness to supporting my husband in whatever way I could. I got a great job in a district I ended up retiring from thirty years later. My husband finished well and was hired by the district he eventually retired from. Our boys were resilient as they transitioned from OKCS school and day care to the school where I taught and to a daycare home that was run by an amazing Christian woman. God provided all along the way. When I opened myself to God's best for me and our family, I was no longer stuck. Diving down and recognizing (and admitting) the depression was an important part of getting back to a place of peace.

I experienced this in a physical sense not too long ago. I was enjoying the warm South Pacific waters in Hawaii. Standing on the shore, feet in the water, thinking about going all in, my feet kept sinking deeper and deeper into the sand. I was becoming rooted in the shallow water, unable to move in any direction. I finally dove in—got totally wet—and enjoyed the full benefits of the ocean. The same is true of God's presence. You must be completely "enslaved" and surrendered to His will & His service to fully understand His presence and joy in your life. Our commitment can't be half-hearted.

In Phil. 1:1-2 Paul starts his greeting by referring to himself and Timothy as "bond-servants of Jesus Christ." As we contemplate what it means to be a slave of Christ, it might have a negative connotation to some. We must remember that we are bound to something. If it is not Christ, it is something else—our work, our insecurities, our fears, an addiction. We can't be "afraid" to be called a servant of God. It is not an unhappy experience of bondage, but a submission of our will that is necessary to bring His plan for our lives to fruition—which will bring great happiness to our hearts. Dive in, get completely wet, and become engulfed in His will. It will give you a **higher ground** perspective.

Another lesson illustrating how God gives us glimpses of His perspective came on a cloudy coastal morning. My husband and I decided to take a hike to a beautiful secluded beach. The trail head started on the mountain side of the coast. Having never been on this path before we had to walk in faith that there was something worthwhile on the other side. We had read the map and the literature, now we had to step out in faith and believe.

Once we crested the top of the hill, we encountered a view of the ocean shrouded in fog. At first, we could see very little—an occasional peak at some blue water or white sand. As the morning made way to early afternoon the fog bank began to dissipate. Now we could see a white beach and crashing waves. Eventually the clouds were far enough back that we were able to partake in a panoramic view of the shoreline—absolutely gorgeous. These glimpses of what was to come kept us moving in the right direction.

In our faith we also catch glimpses of God's kingdom and what is to come. It helps to motivate us to keep going—to persevere for that final reward. There was suffering in that hike—sore muscles, endless uphill climbs, steep and rocky downhill treks, heat, thirst, and exhaustion. Similarly, we experience trials daily that could keep us away from our end reward, but those glimpses of heaven help us to keep on keepin' on.

My spiritual fog-lifting on that Thanksgiving Day was a little glimpse for me of what was ahead. The problems didn't disappear, I just had a new perspective. I Corinthians 13:12 puts it this way, "Now we see but a poor reflection as in a mirror (*or in a fog*); then we shall see face to face." What a glorious day it will be when we see Jesus face-to-face. The fog will be completely lifted and we will know Him in His fullness. There will be no more earthly distractions or pain to veil our understanding or love for God. It will be like that glorious panoramic view of the ocean.

On our way back we had a slightly different view. We had experienced a pristine beach, felt the sand on our toes, and the cool water on our feet. We drank it all in. Now we were back on the top of the hill, dripping in sweat, weary and worn, with only a memory of what we had experienced. This time looking out over the waters' expanse we saw the shoreline, a bank of fog, and past the fog more beautiful blue water—a site that could be seen only through the pain of making the journey back to the top of the mountain.

God allows us to go through suffering, but each time we take a step in faith, He rewards us with a greater and more complete glimpse of Himself and who He is. We experience his blessings and joys and see His goodness. It helps us the next time we need to endure through a tough time. Our remembrances of what God has done for us, even though veiled by fog, encourage us to move forward with Him. Go with God to get a view from the top.

Summing it Up:

- He will never cut Himself off from us. His love does not depend on us. He may even use depression or other trials to bring about good.
- God's Word tells us that healing comes through laying hands on others and praying for them, anointing their heads with oil.
- You must be completely "enslaved" and surrendered to His will and His service to fully understand His presence and joy in your life. Our commitment can't be half-hearted.
- In our faith we also catch glimpses of God's kingdom and what is to come along the way. It helps to motivate us to keep going—to endure for that final reward.

- God allows us to go through suffering, but each time we take a step in faith, He rewards us with a greater and more complete glimpse of Himself and who He is.

☀ Highlights from God's Word:
- Romans 8:28
- James 5:14
- Romans 6:15–18
- 1 Corinthians 13:12
- James 1:12

Memos of Mountaintop Moments

Chapter 5
JOY?...NOW?...HOW?

Consider it pure joy, my brothers, whenever you face trials of many kinds. James 1:2

Every year, Lori carved out a weekend to make a solo trek up the mountain to her family's cabin. It was an annual time to reset and refresh, seek spiritual direction and emotional strength. It was a time to seek **higher ground** while literally being on **higher ground.** God always met her there and affirmed the promise of her favorite verse, "'For I know the plans I have for you,' declares the Lord, 'plans to prosper you and not to harm you, plans to give you hope and a future'" (Jeremiah 29:11).

This year was different. The harrowing year she had just been through had delayed her visit to the cabin. Instead of a reset, she needed rest. She needed a renewal of the joy that had been slowly sucked from her spirit. She needed to be able to breathe deeply of the joy of the Lord. Lori took her Bible and the study God had prompted her to purchase months before, *Fight Back with Joy*[2]. She reflected on what God was trying to teach her through her trials.

Just a year before, in November of 2020, things had started off looking hopeful and optimistic. Lori was at a crossroads. She had been toying with the idea of starting her own business based around wellness and nutrition. She felt like God was saying she could stay where she was and be fine, or she could launch her

---
[2] Feinberg, Margaret. *Fight Back with Joy.* Worthy Books, 2015.

ministry and business and live out God's best for her life. She was scared, but excited about the possibilities.

She and her husband, Ken, had run the numbers for their finances, knowing that she would eventually be leaving a job that paid a six-figure salary. They agreed that she should keep her job one more year. After that, it would be tight, but they could make it work as they waited for her business to take off. She met with a mentor, set up her business plan, and developed a website.***

Lori knew she was taking a leap of faith, but it was with God. She wanted to be all in, honoring God with everything: work, finances, service, and family. As a symbol of their commitment, their family decided to build a neighborhood prayer box in front of their house in early 2021. Lori believed that Satan was not happy about this decision, so she and her family clothed themselves with God's armor, ready to face the potential of spiritual warfare. Satan is out to kill, steal, and destroy, and they were soon to face a battle.

On a fateful day in March, their youngest son, Blake, was watching out the window for a friend to come. Ken and their older son, Seth, were in front of their prayer box with their dog on a leash, ready to take a walk. A neighbor's dog somehow escaped from his leash and came up from behind, attacking their smaller dog, Odie. It happened so quickly. It was totally out of character for this dog, but for some reason his animal nature felt threatened and his instincts took over.

Ken grabbed their dog, bleeding and severely injured, to rush him to the veterinarian's office. At that same time Blake's friend arrived. Lori sent Blake off with his friend, not realizing how traumatized her eight-year-old son was after watching the scene play out in front of him. Already anxious about Covid, Blake began to experience panic attacks, anxiety, and signs of post-traumatic stress disorder (PTSD). He was using negative emotions to cope with life, and over the next few months continued to spiral downward.

Odie required surgery and a long road to recovery, but eventually he came out on top of things. In the meantime, some other wounds needed healing. The neighbor was distraught, offered to pay for the vet bills, and certainly expected a lawsuit, at most, or neighborly tensions, at the least. Lori and Ken realized that the prayer box was an open testimony to the neighborhood about their faith. They treated this neighbor with kindness and forgiveness, assured him that they understood it was not his fault, and refused to let him pay.

In the meantime, Lori began to feel physically drained, but she figured it was a result of the emotional stress of the past few months. By May and June, she was practically bed-ridden. She was barely hanging on at work, unable to give her family her all, and she was having trouble breathing. She was tested for Covid, but her test results came back negative.

In July, she had a teleconference with her doctor. During that call, they decided she should come in for an appointment. She wasn't able to get in until mid-August. At this appointment there was no diagnosis, and the doctor's advice was to just make herself get up every day. The doctor renewed her asthma inhaler prescription, and they made another appointment for a complete physical in October.

In late August and September word came that the forest around their cabin was ablaze. The flames got within five hundred yards of the back of their cabin, closer than any previous fire had ever been before. For many weeks things were touch and go. Lori lost nights of sleep praying for the community and reliving vacation memories at the cabin with her grandparents and other family members.

Stress was mounting, but Lori was determined to keep things as normal as possible. One Saturday morning she got up at dark-thirty to meet her running group. She completely forgot about her work computer being in the trunk. She drove to the meeting place, parked her car, put her purse in the trunk, and joined her partners in training. When she returned to her car, her purse was gone.

Focused on the credit cards and identification theft, it wasn't until she got home that it dawned on her that her work computer and all of her project folders had been stolen as well. Being in the medical field, if any of the patients' medical or personal information was compromised, Lori could lose her job. Never mind that she was going to be quitting at the end of the year. She didn't want to go out like this. It was excruciating as she waited to hear if any of the information had been accessed.

At this point, Lori felt as if God's hand had been removed from her life. She was experiencing personal depression deeper than she had felt in a long time. Her friends were busy with their own problems, Ken was in the middle of a doctoral program, and Blake was continuing to show signs of anxiety. The book and Bible study on joy Lori had bought had sat unopened on her shelf for a couple of months, but at this moment, God prompted her to teach Blake about choosing joy.

Wait! What? Joy? Now? How? She couldn't imagine how she could teach anyone anything, when she was in the middle of more than she could handle herself. Nothing that happened was a life-altering crisis, but the accumulation of trials was overwhelming and joy-sapping.

As the infomercials say, "But wait, there's more!" In October, Lori's visit to the doctor revealed that she had Epstein Barr, a chronic viral infection that most likely was exacerbated by the Covid-19 vaccine. She was actually relieved to know that her symptoms weren't just all in her mind. There really was a reason for her energy drain. Her best course of action was to continue to take care of herself with healthy eating and increased exercising.

Finding time for self-care was almost impossible as she continued to juggle three jobs, support her husband's schooling, play taxi to the boys' schools and activities, and train a new puppy (Odie needed a buddy). On top of all that, she found herself quarantined with the rest of the family as her oldest son and husband tested positive for Covid.

At the beginning of November 2021, Lori got word that her grandma was in her last days. She was being kept comfortable through hospice. Just a few days later, on Blake's birthday, Lori got the call that her grandmother had passed. Blake was practicing some of the coping skills that Lori was trying to teach him, but she was concerned that this would push him over the edge. He had an especially close relationship with his great grandma.

The Covid hiatus finally ended. Lori was back to driving the boys everywhere. One morning, on her way home from dropping off their high schooler, she got a call that he had left his baseball bag in the car. She turned the car around and ended up behind a driver that had no business being on the road. Lori cautiously stopped at a stop sign, waited for the woman in front of her to turn right, paused as an on-coming truck passed by, and eased into her own turn. She instantly connected with the woman's bumper ahead of her as she had come to a complete, abrupt stop in the middle of the intersection.

The ensuing fender bender was mild. No one was hurt. There was no damage to either car. But it was the proverbial last straw that broke the camel's back. The water works started. Lori even entertained a momentary thought that if she just drove herself into a brick wall, all of this pain would go away. It was this thought, which she quickly brought captive to the Lord, that made her realize it was past time to get up to her cabin.

The time with God was a soothing balm to her soul. In between napping, Lori finished the entire Bible study on joy in the few short days she was there. She realized she was doing a lot of the things necessary to "fight back with joy," but she was not claiming God's promises, clinging to Him for her peace and hope, nor focusing on the goodness of God in her life.

Looking back at the year she realized that God's hand had been with her all along. She listed her blessings: 1) Both the dog and their relationship with their neighbor healed. 2) The showering of grace they bestowed upon their neighbor opened up opportunities to share more of Christ. 3) The flames had come close, but the cabin had been saved. 4) The thieves were never able to access the database on her computer, so an unhappy ending to her job was averted.

Even Blake was making progress. God had used Lori's background, experience, and personal life lessons to help bring about his healing. The death of her grandmother and the fear that Blake would be adversely affected was resolved. God knew and understood, and His plan was to use Blake's grieving as part of his healing. Attending the memorial service actually helped him to face some of his anxieties and release some of his fears about death.

Lori realized that joy was not a feeling. Joy was being in a place of peace and freedom, knowing that God is in control, in spite of the circumstances. She received a new purpose and made a plan to serve others and to look for ways that God was revealing Himself to her. She began to feel excitement again about her life, her business, and her calling.

Who would have known that the trials we face could culminate in learning to embrace God-given joy in our lives? Sometimes we feel like He has removed His presence from us. That is exactly when He is preparing us to trust Him more and lean on Him completely. When we finally cling to Him, claim His promises, and fulfill His call to serve others, we can experience **joy**, **now**, exactly **how** He intended.

***You can find out more about Lori Tolleson's new business on her website at http://tollesonnutrition.com or follow Tolleson Nutrition Consulting on Facebook.

⬆ Summing it Up:
- When we trust God, sometimes we must take a leap of faith to follow His best plan for us.
- Satan is out to steal and kill and destroy. We must be prepared for spiritual warfare.
- The showering of God's grace on others, the same grace that he extended to each of us, opens up relationships and brings blessings beyond our imaginations.
- Sometimes we feel like God has removed His presence from us. That is exactly when He is preparing us to trust Him more and lean on Him completely. When we finally cling to Him, claim His promises, and fulfill His call to serve others, we can experience joy, now, exactly how He intended.

☀ Highlights from God's Word:
- Jeremiah 29:11
- John 10:10; Ephesians 6:10-18
- Colossians 3:12-13; John 13:34-35
- James 1:2-4

Memos of Mountaintop Moments

Chapter 6
DON'T FIGHT THE FLIGHT

Do not be afraid or discouraged because of this vast army. For the battle is not yours, but God's. 2 Chronicles 20:15b

The Wright Brothers, Wilbur and Orville, are a fascinating pair. They grew up in a family who loved to think and talk about deep and often controversial topics. Their family encouraged hard work, and yet delighted in experimenting and tinkering. Wilbur invented a machine that would help fold his father's church bulletins. The two brothers together opened a print shop in which they were constantly trying to improve the printing process. They eventually opened a bike shop. Their excitement about the fun of cycling drove them to create better gears and braking mechanisms for the bicycles that everyone around Dayton, Ohio, was riding.

One thing Wilbur and Orville shared was their dream of flying. They flew kites, studied birds' wing movements, and researched wind patterns. Combining this with their knowledge of bike-building, they began to experiment with creating gliders. They eventually traveled to Kitty Hawk, North Carolina, where there were strong, steady winds and open space. It was here they would try out their flying machines. A quick glance might have you surmising that they built, they experimented, and they flew; thus, we have the airplane! A deeper look would prove that they faced danger, discouragement, and multiple obstacles.

The shifting sand dunes at Kitty Hawk were very problematic throughout their experimenting years. There was no easy access for them to transport all of their equipment. They had multiple failures and crashes. There was no limit to the number of times they went back to the drawing board to rethink their formulas, designs, and wind tunnel models.

Once a successful glider was created, they began work on an airplane. On December 17, 1903, Oroville made the first successful flight. It lasted twelve minutes and covered 120 feet of ground. Though North Carolina's state motto is "First in Flight," this first success was only the beginning.

Back in Ohio, the brothers obtained permission from a local farmer to use his pasture land for further experimentation. They used each crash to learn how to warp the wings for better turns, fiddle with the elevator mechanisms for better lift, and utilize the right materials for balance and structure. By October, 1905, their longest flight was now thirty-nine minutes and twenty-four miles. They could fly straight, turn in circles, and make graceful arcs.

Over the next few years, the fame of the Wright Brothers spread. Their obstacles now came with trying to maintain a business, selling their planes, and dealing with competitors trying to steal their ideas. They eventually received their first orders and were able to celebrate.

Wilbur died an untimely death from contracting an illness while traveling. For Orville, it was too difficult to carry on without his brother and partner. He sold the company, but he continued to tinker with small inventions the rest of his life. Most of the things he invented in his later years were creature comforts for his large house. He created plumbing, heating, and electrical systems that were state-of-the-art. He was especially proud of his built-in vacuum and the homemade book holder on his favorite overstuffed easy chair that could be shifted from side to side.

The Wright Brothers have been celebrated and memorialized as much or more than their countrymen like Washington, Jefferson, and Lincoln. In Tom Crouch's biography of *The Bishop's Boys* he describes these famed inventors:

> "The mythic stature attained by the brothers reflected the nature of their achievement. The airplane was not simply a bit of new technology; it was something akin to a miracle. Flight symbolized the most basic human yearnings. To fly was to achieve freedom, control, power, and an escape from restraint.
>
> "And the invention came from such an unexpected quarter. The Wrights had no special training in science or engineering. While both were well educated, neither had completed the formal coursework required for his high school diploma. Before the summer of 1899, they seemed the most ordinary of men.
>
> "...They were the quintessential Americans, whose success seemed compounded of hard work, perseverance, and common sense, with a liberal dollop of Yankee ingenuity—raised to the level of genius."[3]

To highlight some observations regarding their accomplishments:

---

[3] Crouch, Tom. *The Bishop's Boys, A Life of Wilbur and Orville Wright.* W.W. Norton & Company Ltd., 2003. P. 504.

- They were underqualified, uneducated, and unlikely to succeed
- They experienced multiple failures
- Their failures became the drawing ground for their next plan
- They persevered at every stage
- Their achievement was akin to a miracle

God loves to perform miracles through the most unlikely of people and circumstances. It doesn't take long to look through the Old and New Testaments to find that the men and women He used were underqualified, uneducated, and unlikely candidates for the job. Moses stuttered. David was a common shepherd. Peter was an uneducated fisherman. Mary Magdalene was a woman who had been demon-possessed. Paul was a murderer of Christians.

God took these "lowly" humans to **higher ground** by giving them purpose and rewarding their perseverance. They all experienced failure along the way. Peter denied Christ—three times, for "Pete's" sake. He was eventually able to take his failures to the Upper Room, where the disciples awaited the infilling of the Holy Spirit. Through prayer and perseverance, Peter became a powerful preacher of the gospel of Christ to Jews and Gentiles alike. His achievements were miraculous workings of God.

If we studied all of these ordinary people from Biblical times and followed them from their humble beginnings to their saintly status, we would find that we could add one more quality to the previous list.

- They were humble before God and let Him fight their battles

A perfect example of this is found in 2 Chronicles. King Jehoshaphat became ruler of Judah at age thirty-five. In his early years, Jehoshaphat walked in the ways of King David, consulting the God of his father and following His commands. By staying in tune with God, Jehoshaphat got rid of the idols of the land, ruled wisely, and recognized when circumstances were beyond his control.

When King Jehoshaphat was told that a vast army was coming against him, he declared fasting and prayer throughout the land. The people of Judah came from every town to seek the Lord. King Jehoshaphat's prayer in 2 Chronicles 20:6-12 gives us great insight into his success. First, King Jehoshaphat reminded his people of God's greatness, His unlimited power, and His promises. The key to the prayer comes at the end when he says, "For we have no power to face this vast army that is attacking us. We do not know what to do, but our eyes are upon you" (2 Chronicles 20:12b).

So often we start our prayers with letting God know how we plan to "help" Him fix the problem. A devotion by Rick Warren illustrated the futility of trying to do things our way. He commented on how ridiculous it would be to flap our arms faster and faster to help an ascending plane get off the ground, but that's what we often do. We think it's up to us to figure it out and fight the flight. Pastor Rick aptly states, "People tend toward independence, and so when you see a problem, you think, 'I've got to figure this out. It's up to me!' You assume God's role, and it wears you out, because you were never meant to carry it in the first place."[4]

---

[4] Warren, R. (2021, September 10). *Maybe it's Time to Give Up.* Pastor Rick's Daily Hope. https://pastorrick.com/maybe-its-time-to-give-up/

King Jehoshaphat figured out what Paul came to realize in his missionary journeys and his commitment to doing God's work. As Paul was pleading with the Lord to take away his "thorn in the flesh," the Lord said to him, "My grace is sufficient for you, for my power is made perfect in weakness" (2 Corinthians 12:9). Admitting we are powerless without the help of Christ is a huge step in experiencing a miracle-filled existence. God wants to use our weakness to display His strength.

After King Jehoshaphat's prayer, the spirit of the Lord came upon a Levite named Jahaziel. He gave them the plan of attack: March down to where the army is advancing. Take up your positions, but stand firm and watch how the Lord will deliver you. Don't be discouraged or afraid for the Lord will be with you (see 2 Chronicles 20:15-17).

This declaration was met with praise and worship. The praise band was commissioned to lead the army with their singing. As they sang and praised the Almighty God, the Lord set ambushes against the enemy armies, and they began to fight each other. King Jehoshaphat's army did not have to lift a sword. Instead, when they reached the valley, all they could see were the defeated soldiers. They set about collecting the plunder for three days. On the fourth day they assembled to praise the Lord for the victory. Praise both preceded and followed triumph.

We can't imagine the Wright Brothers attempting to flap their arms as they were launching their first planes. It would have been equally useless for King Jehoshaphat's army to have launched into an all-out fight with the massive armies before them. We can use these stories to apply truths to our own daily living.

Don't let your qualifications, or lack thereof, keep you from obeying God and allowing Him to work through your talents, abilities, and especially your weaknesses. When (not if) you fail, let God help you redeem your failures into successes that will thwart the enemy's plans. Persevere when times get tough. Our perseverance helps us become mature and complete in character. Recognize your weaknesses, and admit that you do not know what to do. Surrender your life with its inevitable problems to God so that He can fight the battles for you. Then you will be able to recognize and praise the One who brings about each miracle.

Don't fight the flight. Put your flapping arms down. Let God be the one to lift you to **higher ground.**

Summing it Up:
- God loves to perform miracles through the most unlikely of people and circumstances.
- When praying about a problem, recognize God's goodness and power, then admit that you do not know what to do and that you are depending on Him.
- God wants to use our weakness to display His strength.
- Praise should both precede and follow triumph.
- Persevere when times get tough because perseverance helps us become mature and complete in character.

Highlights from God's Word:
- Philippians 4:13
- 2 Chronicles 20:6-12
- 2 Corinthians 12:9
- Hebrews 13:15
- James 1:4

Memos of Mountaintop Moments

Chapter 7
A HEAVENLY PLANTING

So neither he who plants nor he who waters is anything, but only God, who makes things grow. 1 Corinthians 3:7

Jenn stepped off the plane, welcoming a chance to stretch her legs after the long flight from Honolulu to Los Angeles. The quick break preceded the final phase of her journey to a week of collaboration and encouragement with fellow-authors. This mountain retreat would be a perfect place to put distractions aside and concentrate on her craft. She couldn't wait.

Unlike other flights that Jenn was used to, the connecting forty-minute ride from LAX to Sacramento did not have assigned seats. It was a choose-your-own, hope-there-is-something-decent-available opportunity. As she made her way down the aisle, Jenn scrutinized the choices still at her disposal and assessed the passengers already seated. Jenn made eye contact with a businessman, probably in his late fifties or early sixties.

"May I sit next to you?" she asked, as she pointed to the seat next to him. She knew she didn't technically have to ask his permission, but she felt it was the respectful thing to do.

"Sure," he replied. They then did the somewhat awkward dance of arranging bodies and baggage into the not-so-spacious accommodations.

As a further gesture of politeness and thanks for allowing her to take up the neighboring space, Jenn introduced herself and asked the gentleman his name and what he did for a living. His name was Ken, and he was surprisingly up for a bit of conversation. The ease of communicating with someone from the next generation came naturally for Jenn, so they jumped into a back-and-forth dialogue that covered surface information. Eventually their banter got deeper and more insightful.

Jenn soon found out that Ken, a retired military officer, traveled the country training cadets and instructors in local high school ROTC programs. He shared his passion about providing these leaders with a clear path to embracing discipline and direction in their lives. Knowing that not all of the military students had positive role models or father figures, Ken attempted to balance his high expectations with a true concern for their well-being.

After answering some of Jenn's questions about his line of work, he wanted to know more about what she did. She explained that she was a writer and an on-line and podcast communicator who loves to encourage families. She told him a little bit about the retreat she was attending, and his interest was piqued.

Ken talked about wishing he could write a book, and what an elusive goal that seemed to be for him. He immediately expressed self-doubt based on past learning barriers. Jenn encouraged him to go for it. He had a lot of experience and expertise regarding solid leadership principles, and perhaps he could even voice-dictate his thoughts. She urged him to think about using his unique abilities and talents.

Maybe because he wanted to get the focus off of himself, Ken asked Jenn to tell him more about her writing subject. She told him that she encourages mothers to know that they are strong enough to be good mothers. In a world where there are hundreds of opinions about how to be the best parent, moms get confused about how to do it right. They are often discouraged and frustrated in their own abilities to raise their children properly. Jenn offers hope and grace to help moms see that they are already doing many things well.

As she was sharing all of this, Ken's wheels were turning. He began to tell of his three adult daughters. Two girls were from his first marriage, the third daughter was from his second marriage. His youngest daughter, he proudly reported, was driven and successful. He worried about the other two. His first wife was opposed to things of faith. He could see evidence of depression and hopelessness in their lives as a result of not having a belief in God.

Ken began to reflect on the fact that his first wife had been involved with consulting psychics and mediums. He paused for a moment before asking Jenn, "What do you know about that? Do you know anything about the spirit world?"

The seeds of God's heavenly garden, Ken's heart, were being tended throughout the conversation. Jenn took a moment to breathe in a prayer asking the Holy Spirit to help her till and water the soil. Here was a golden opportunity to unfold God's truth, but she wanted to express it in a way that would make sense and tie in with the need that this man had. Ken desperately wanted to be able to connect with his daughters, and he wanted to be able to bridge the gap with communication and love. It seemed evident that Ken knew that there was something beyond ourselves that his daughters were missing, and he was seeking answers and direction.

Jenn's silent prayer took but a moment, but the Holy Spirit transcended time and helped clear her thoughts. She began by sharing that she believed there was a very real spiritual realm. We were all created to worship something, and answers could come from a variety of directions as we sought to fill that void.

She then shared that the main difference between Christianity and other religions or cultic practices like those Ken had described was that the God of the Bible wants to know us personally. He gives us the free-will to choose Him because He isn't a puppet master or a dictator.

Jenn began to use military language to help Ken relate to what she was saying. She said she believed we have an enemy. The best thing Ken could do to fight for his girls was to pray for them, that they would come to know God. She went on to tell Ken about the God of the Bible, who is bigger than us. He is holy, righteous, just, and loving. It doesn't matter what we've done or not done in this life because we all matter to Him, and He hears us.

Jenn expressed confidence that through Ken's prayers, God would put someone in the paths of Ken's daughters to draw them to Him. Ken could let the God, who knows and sees all, work out the details. Whether it was through their kids' daycare, at the gas station, or on their jobs, Ken could pray that someone would be placed in their lives to show them who God is.

The flow of conversation had been natural and organic. Jenn had been very conscious of not wanting to be pushy or presumptuous.

She had tried to practice good listening skills. At this point in the flight, Ken's demeanor became thoughtful and he appeared close to tears. He paused to breathe in and out a few times.

Then he said, "Can I ask you a question? Why did you choose to sit here?"

Jenn just grinned and replied, "It was open and you seemed like a nice guy."

She knew that God had set up this divine appointment. She breathed a prayer of thanksgiving as the plane began its final descent. Ken expressed his thankfulness for her time and attention. It was evident that his thoughts were swirling, and he was trying to make sense of this encounter and the deep spiritual stirrings within. They walked off the plane together to the luggage carousel for baggage claim.

As they parted, Jenn was overwhelmed that God had used her for this Heavenly planting. She knew that this side of Heaven she would probably never know how the seeds of their conversation would be cultivated. It hadn't been her job to bring Ken to a place of commitment. She had just been obedient to give of her time and spiritual insights!

Jenn later reflected how amazing God was. There was no way she could have manipulated or controlled this encounter. The limited time frame of the flight was perfect for an urgent message to be delivered. Her recent study of the names of God had been fresh on her heart and mind, allowing her to share her beliefs with confidence. The exact seat at this exact time had been "assigned" long before the flight had been scheduled.

The harvest is plentiful; in other words, there are opportunities always before us. We can look at people as interruptions and annoyances, or we can ask God to go before us and prepare us to see and hear them as He does. Jesus was the prime example of making space for others throughout the Gospels. He took time to make sure the hungry crowds had been fed. He changed directions to go with the synagogue ruler whose daughter was ill. He welcomed the children who were brought to Him. He stopped to heal a man who had been blind since birth.

It is a relief to know that we don't have to be in charge of making the garden grow. Some of us will plant, others will water, according to the task God has given us. Only God can make it grow. We just have to be poised with openness to listen to God's voice. We have the privilege of sharing the hope and love of God with others, and we don't have to be flying in the clouds to do it. God can bring a **higher ground** opportunity before us anytime, anywhere.

Summing it Up:

- The harvest is plentiful; in other words, there are opportunities always before us to share the hope and love of God with others.
- Jesus was the prime example for us to make space for others.
- Some of us will plant, others will water, but only God can make it grow.

☀ Highlights from God's Word

- Luke 10:2
- Crowds were fed—Matthew 15:29-39
- Jairus' daughter was healed—Mark 5:21-42
- Children were welcomed—Luke 18:15-16
- Blind man was healed—John 9:1-12
- I Corinthians 3:6-9

Memos of Mountaintop Moments

Chapter 8
THE LORD'S TIMING

With the Lord a day is like a thousand years, and a thousand years are like a day. 2 Peter 3:8b

"We fly about 1000 hours a year," Mark explained. That sounded like a pretty sweet deal, averaging approximately twenty hours a week. However, he went on to say that those hours did not include the layover time or the hours spent traveling to the departure airport. Regardless of the time spent on the road or in the sky, Mark felt like those annual required hours always flew by so quickly. He is one of those lucky people who still loves what they do, even after twenty-five plus years in the profession.

A thousand hours might seem to pass by rapidly when you are doing what you love, but the time it took for Mark's dream to come true probably seemed like an eternity to a youngster. From his earliest memories, Mark knew he wanted to be a pilot. His desire to be on **higher ground**, flying above the clouds, was apparent from the time he was about two. Mark's dad was a corporate pilot, so Mark was always looking up at planes, believing it was his dad flying by each time. One day, Mark's mom took him to the airport to watch his dad leave on a trip. Mark, just a toddler at the time, told his mom, "I'm going to take you flying someday." This was, apparently, his first complete sentence.

Mark was more than just a little boy with a pipe dream that would someday change as he grew older. He never even considered any other career, and God certainly paved the way for him to fulfill his dream. Mark got his pilot's license when he was seventeen years old. His mom, as Mark had promised fifteen years earlier, got to be his first passenger.

Mark's pursuit of a college major at Cal State University, Bakersfield, had one purpose. He needed a college degree to be hired for any type of corporate or commercial flying. He chose the major he could complete with the fewest required credits, and he finished his courses in three and a half years. By the time he was twenty-two, Mark was co-piloting charter and corporate jets. Ironically he wasn't old enough to book a rental car at their layovers, but he was allowed to fly a multi-million-dollar Learjet. Through the years Mark moved from corporate and charter aviation to eventually flying for Alaska Airlines. He has been with them for the past nineteen years, and he was recently promoted to captain.

Early in his career, as a co-pilot, Mark had a lot of time, one thousand hours as mentioned earlier, to talk to the captains he flew with. Mark remembers a particular pilot he was paired with quite often. This gentleman had never been married. He took advantage of his single status at each layover to go to clubs and meet women. Mark chose to use his time differently—seeing sights, playing basketball, or taking some time to read and rest.

One day, while they were cruising at a high altitude, the pilot had been sharing some of his exploits from the previous stop. He looked at Mark and said, "You probably just think I'm a heathen going to hell, don't you?"

A little taken aback, Mark replied, "Well, I'm not the judge, and I don't have the right to make that decision."

The pilot replied, "I can't believe you just said that. Every Christian I've known thinks I'm the worst person in the world. They don't want anything to do with me, but you just keep talking to me and hanging out with me."

Mark explained, "As a Christian, I'm supposed to show you love and grace and just be here for you."

From that point on, the door was opened to talk about deeper things. The pilot knew he wouldn't be judged by Mark and he felt comfortable asking probing questions and discussing topics on a spiritual level. He didn't make a decision for Christ during the years Mark was flying with him, but the seeds were planted, and this gentleman saw Christ living in Mark.

It is so important to live our lives as believers in Jesus without casting judgment on others or putting on a front of perfection. We need to show love and grace to those who have not yet made a decision to live for the Lord, because that is exactly what the Lord did for us. We need to remember that we are all broken and have a need for a Savior. Pretending like we have always had everything together might be the reason someone resists Christianity. It is our humble, open spirit that points others to Christ. Max Lucado said it so eloquently.

> "'I'm so glad I'm not like *that*,' we tell ourselves. But the truth is we are *all* hypocrites. We have all deceived others by hiding our sin. We have all worshiped God with the same mouth that judges others. Until we acknowledge who we really are—sinners in need of grace—we will always struggle with deception. Until we adopt the mindset of the

tax collector In Jesus' parable who said, 'God have mercy on me, a sinner' (Luke 18:13), we will never experience the humility that God desires us to have. So today, let's leave the acting for Hollywood and humbly accept our brokenness. For when we do, we will have hearts that bring honor to God."[5]

Another captain that Mark often co-piloted with made a comment one day that had Mark wondering at first whether his life was shining for Christ like he thought. They were shooting the breeze, talking about life, when Mark mentioned something about working with the youth group at church. The captain looked at him, and with surprise and a little disbelief in his tone he said, "Wait, you're a Christian?"

Mark immediately thought over what he might have said or done to make this guy question his faith. It hit him like a ton of bricks. Seeing Mark's confused, hurt look, the captain went on to explain. "It's just that you're nice to the gay flight attendants. Actually, you're nice to everyone! I've never met a Christian that isn't judgmental, sneering at those they disapprove of behind their backs. I just never thought you were a Christian because of how you treated people."

Mark was able to relax a bit, but he was also saddened to think that so many people see Christians as judgmental and uncaring. That is the exact opposite of what we are called to be. He shared with this captain the reason he treats everyone with love and respect is because of what Jesus did for us. Christ not only modeled living a life of love for your neighbor, He died so that we all could be saved. Not only did Mark's attitude toward others act as a

---

[5] Lucado, Max. *Ten Women of the Bible Study Guide.* Nashville, Tennessee: Thomas Nelson, 2016.

witness, but it opened up an opportunity for him to explain the hope he had in the Lord that enabled him to live that way.

Mark has shared this incident with some of the kids in the youth group. It perfectly illustrates that others are watching our actions, even when we are unaware of it. How we treat others is a witness whether we realize it or not. Along with that, we need to be ready to give the reason for our hope (see 1 Peter 3:15)

In regards to this, Mark mentioned this quote attributed to St. Francis of Assisi: "Preach the gospel at all times. Use words when necessary." Mark agrees with author, Kevin Harney, who says, "I understand the spirit of this quote, and I think it makes a good point. But in some cases, people use it as an excuse to avoid articulating their faith...If I could, I would change the quote to read: 'Preach the gospel at all times—and there will *always* be a point when words are necessary.'"[6]

We need to live a balance of being salt and light in our world, while also being ready to share the Good News of salvation. If we live a great life before our neighbors and friends but never tell them that they can have assurance of eternal life, we are not fulfilling the commission that Jesus gave us.

Most of the pilots that Mark flew with remained acquaintances, but one particular captain became a life-long friend. The two men were close in age and started their families at about the same time. Their wives taught together for a period of time. They celebrated the births of each other's children and attended their baptisms and dedications.

---

[6] Harney, Kevin G. (2009). *Organic Outreach for Ordinary People*. Grand Rapids, Michigan: Zondervan, p. 220.

Mark and his wife, Julia, were open about their faith, and their friends were supportive of what the Schaefers believed and stood for. The friends' faith, however, was a bit more ambiguous. They were both raised Catholic, but they didn't really practice their religion on a regular basis. Besides going to mass on Christmas and Easter and attending Catholic weddings and funerals, there wasn't much "meat" to their faith.

In 2015 these friends moved to Texas due to a change in jobs. Their boys, now teenagers, started going to a local youth group where many of their friends attended. They were part of the summer youth camps, and church was a priority in the boys' lives.

Mark recently paid these friends a visit while making a transaction on a new truck he was purchasing in their town. Although he was exhausted from flying all night and experiencing jet lag, he soon became energized with the changes he was seeing in his friend and the depth of their conversation regarding faith. His friend and his wife had actually attended a few services at the church their boys were going to. They were excited about the services and the people they met.

These friends had started listening to a daily podcast leading them through the Bible in a year. As they were discussing their summer calendar, family vacations, and the boys' sports schedules, it was evident that they were making sure that the week for church camp was blocked out and saved for the youth event. Mark's friend asked Mark about finding some Christian music groups he could listen to in the car, as he was trying to keep himself surrounded with a positive atmosphere throughout the day.

Mark noted that their friends had experienced some trauma in the past couple of years, but they seemed to have a peace and hope that had not been there in the past. This friendship of over twenty-four years was taking on a new level. The many conversations of the past where Mark and Julia were able to share about their love for Jesus and the many prayers they had prayed for their friends were beginning to come to fruition.

We would like for everyone to change in an instant, but God allows just the right amount of time for them to process and come to a place of readiness to accept Him. He is not slow, but is patient, wooing each one to come to Himself and seek repentance. He uses you and me. He uses the seeds we plant through living our lives as Jesus did. He uses children attending youth groups. He uses long-term close friendships and fellowship. When we see the fruit beginning to yield a harvest, it is so exciting.

Mark and Julia exuded this excitement as they told of these recent events. Their joy superseded the heights when Mark is actually in the sky flying. A thousand flying hours may seem like a moment to Mark, and a moment may seem like a thousand hours. Likewise, God continues His work patiently, not wanting anyone to perish. His days are like a thousand years, and a thousand years are like a day. His timing is perfect.

Summing it Up:

- We must recognize that we are all sinners in need of grace. Our humble acceptance of our brokenness brings honor and glory to God and draws others to the Christ living in us.

- How we treat others is a witness whether we realize it or not. We need to be ready to give the reason for our hope.
- We need to be salt and light in our world. We also need to be obedient to Jesus' commission to "tell" the world about Him.
- We would like for everyone to change in an instant, but God allows just the right amount of time for them to process and come to a place of readiness to accept Him.

☀ Highlights from God's Word:

- Romans 3:22-24
- 1 Peter 3:15
- Matthew 5:13-16; Matthew 28:18-20
- 2 Peter 3:8-9

Memos of Mountaintop Moments

Chapter 9
THE LOFT

From the fullness of his grace we have all received one blessing after another. John 1:16

A while back, I attended a conference with one of my dear friends. We had agreed to share a hotel room, and in an effort to save some money, she booked the hotel through a third-party that offered a big discount. The pictures of the inn were warm and inviting. The reviews were good (perhaps submitted by the owner's relatives), and the hotel was not too far from our conference venue. We prattled and shared during our car ride to San Jose, California, anticipating a good night's sleep before our first day of learning.

When we first arrived, we were a little concerned about the location of the hotel in the city. It was a bit isolated, tucked into an industrial area, with a few unsavory characters passing by occasionally. A lady clad in a skin-tight leopard body suit was waiting for someone in the door of her downstairs room. Soon, a cowboy-hat wearing "gentleman" in a two-ton truck arrived for their rendezvous. Ignoring the red flags, and since it was still daylight, we checked in and headed up to our second-story room. There was no elevator, so we lugged our suitcases, our laptops, and any valuables that we were concerned about leaving in the car, to our "cozy" space. More warning signs appeared as we passed by several pails catching water drips from the window-unit air conditioners.

The room was just as piece-meal as the condensation solutions had been. There were cords running along the ceiling and floors to plugs whose contacts had worn out long ago. Any attempt to plug in our cell phones, hair dryers, or computers was met with disappointment. The curtains hung half-way off the rods, wall paper pieces were peeling away from the wall, and the beds were not attached to the headboards. The small refrigerator was equipped with a coffee maker on top. The problem was that the top-of-fridge height was too tall for the coffee pot cord to reach the plug (which probably wouldn't have worked anyway!). We had to put the coffee pot tray and cups onto the floor in order to make a cup of joe.

To top things off, I woke up with a massive migraine about 4:00 in the morning. I'm not sure if the room bore some particle I was allergic to (visible or invisible), or if I had eaten something that triggered the pain, or if I was feeling the stress of what was to come. Regardless, I was looking forward to a nice hot shower to loosen up the nerve endings in my head. After running the water for several minutes, I realized there was no warm water to be had.

We called down to the front desk, only to be assured that someone would be up to check on it later in the day. Before we left for our workshop, we tried to cancel the reservation for the remainder of the two days, only to find out we would not be refunded since it had been booked through a third party. We decided, reluctantly, to tough it out. We had not planned to eat breakfast in the lobby, but we were glad we had made other plans. The "continental" breakfast plan was a couple of vending machines.

We stopped by a Starbucks for a caffeine fix and a bite to eat. My headache subsided. The conference was wonderful. Exhausted from our day of receiving so much information and valuable tips, we had dinner and drove back to the "Bates Motel." We made sure we were locked and secured on all fronts. We were assured the water situation had been taken care of, so my roommate decided to take her shower before bed. Her screams were the first indication that the fixed warm water problem had not been remedied at all. She felt so bad about the entire fiasco, and she did her best to get the management to understand our frustration. They would not even give us a small refund!

Somehow, we were able to concentrate enough to prepare our homework for the next day. We made the best of the frustrating situation, continued to enjoy each other's company, and reveled in the amazing things we were learning throughout the conference. As soon as we knew there could be no retaliation and were far enough away from the hotel and the city, we placed our review. Suffice it to say, it was not five stars!

I enjoyed one night back in my own bed before heading to Long Beach to support another friend in a huge conference she was in charge of, as CEO of her non-profit organization. I had booked a Hilton on a coupon we had received from a previous incentive stay with the hotel chain. I took my luggage, by elevator, to an eighth-floor room. My room was large and comfortable. There were multiple plugs that worked gloriously. The bed was adorned with fluffy pillows and soft linens. The curtains had the typical blackout shades to pull for complete and secure privacy. The bathroom was well equipped with towels, lovely smelling shampoo and lotion, a hair dryer, and HOT water!

I felt like I was experiencing a little bit of Heaven. The next morning, I went to the restaurant for my complimentary breakfast. It was called The Loft, located on the second floor above the lobby, with a view of Long Beach Harbor. I had made it to **higher ground!** I was handed a menu, and received white table cloth service. Coffee was poured for me from a silver carafe. I ordered one of my favorites, avocado toast and a poached egg. I had a great conversation with my waiter, who had worked there for eleven years. He made me feel right at home. It was an experience in direct contrast to the one just a few days prior.

Sometimes we settle for less than God intends for our lives. I'm not talking about hotels now. I'm talking about the things that draw us because they look good from the outside, don't seem to have much cost, and woo us with false advertising. We feel stuck because we have already made a commitment. It might be a relationship, a job, or a decision we have made. It might be a false sense of who we are or who God is. It might be the lies we have believed about ourselves: "You are not enough." "You are too much." "If only you were _____."

God wants to bring us up and out of those lies. He reveals to us that we are worth the fancy hotel and the hot shower! He feeds us from His banquet table and openly declares His love for us (see Song of Songs 2:4). God knows that sometimes our decisions have brought us to the place we currently reside. His grace and forgiveness release us from the self-inflicted obligation of staying there! He wants us to experience abundant blessings through His love and faithfulness. God knows that sometimes our circumstances are like a dilapidated room that we have not chosen for ourselves. His faithfulness and goodness free us from dwelling in that place.

He provides a safe refuge, and He clothes us with fine things (see Psalm 90:1 and Isaiah 61:10).

I attended a couple sessions at the Long Beach summit, but I had not been able to connect with my friend. She was busy running around, making sure everything was going smoothly, welcoming guest speakers, and fielding questions. I walked back to my hotel room and breathed a quick prayer before checking out. "Lord, if you want me to connect with my friend, make it clear to me what to do next."

I had an immediate sense that I was to return to the venue. I quickly checked my luggage at the front desk for later retrieval and headed back to the symposium center. As I entered the large doors, the first person I saw was my friend. God had answered my prayer. She was on a short break, and invited me to a seating nook, away from the crowds. She let me know how much she appreciated my coming, and shared with me some major prayer requests. We took a moment to let God's kingdom come into our space as we lifted prayers for each other to His throne. With grateful tears and love, we hugged each other and said our farewells.

On my drive home, I reflected on God's goodness. This was a friend I had met in a divine encounter on an airplane a year earlier (see Chapter 6, "I Will Not Be Shaken," in *Solid Ground*). Our circles of friends and influence are polar opposites, but our love for Christ unites us. Our relationship is primarily that of prayer partners. I was so grateful for being able to see her in person earlier in the day.

That is how God works. He takes us from the lowly to the lofty. He meets us at our point of need and brings people into our paths to encourage and support us. He unites unlikely people because of

His own extravagant, unbiased love—love that He has lavished on us.

⬆ Summing it Up:
- God reveals to us that we are worth the fancy hotel and the hot shower! He feeds us from His banquet table and openly declares His love for us.
- God's grace and forgiveness release us from the self-inflicted obligation of staying in the mire of our poor decisions! He wants us to experience abundant blessings through His love and faithfulness.
- God provides a safe refuge, and He clothes us with fine things.
- God unites unlikely people because of His own extravagant, unbiased love—love that He has lavished on us.

☀ Highlights from God's Word:
- Song of Songs 2:4
- John 1:16
- Psalm 90:1; Isaiah 61:10
- 1 John 3:1

Memos of Mountaintop Moments

Chapter 10
GIVE ME THE HILL COUNTRY

Now give me this hill country that the Lord promised me that day. Joshua 14:12a

If someone were to ask you what the best years of your life have been thus far, you would probably reflect on a great moment of success, an amazing vacation, or a powerful and fulfilling relationship. From a spiritual perspective, it might be a wonderful answer to prayer or leading a person into a personal relationship with Christ.

Dan Anderson had many of those best-of-the-best moments. He successfully went through college and seminary, preaching the gospel to many. He was miraculously healed from a disease called Myasthenia Gravis, an auto-immune disorder in which antibodies destroy the communication between nerves and muscles. Dan experienced muscle weakness, double vision, and loss of weight. A healing prayer took all of those things away.

Dan was also successful in the business world...until he wasn't. When it was discovered that some of the clients' investments had been mishandled, he found himself owning up to the mistakes. He took the fall for the rest of the company, while others who were equally or at greater fault avoided conviction. Knowing he must tell the truth, his testimony at trial was enough to bring him a fifteen-year prison sentence, which ended up being twelve years served.

Dan and his wife, Carol (see another one of Carol's miracle stories in Chapter 3), had been praying for a God-given ministry. They wanted their lives to be used for God in amazing ways. They had prayed for victory, for God to give them the hill country, the best years of their lives. They had NOT prayed for a prison sentence! Yet, looking back, they describe the years with Dan behind physical bars as some of the best and most fruitful times of their lives and ministry. God answered their prayers, just not the way man would have thought best. God's ways are higher and better than ours, and we can trust Him for that always! God has a plan for all of us based on His goodness, not on our greatness.

Dan was placed in Taft Correctional Institution, a four-to-five-hour trip from where the Anderson's lived. It is in the hill country forty-seven miles west of Bakersfield. Carol visited every weekend as a way to honor and support her husband. She always made it a point to dress nice and wear a big smile. She thought she was doing this to be an encouragement to her husband, and it did lift his spirits. What Carol didn't know was the impact it was having on the other wives that were also there to visit their husbands.

God was building a ministry of encouragement in the most unlikely place. A smile and saying, "Have a blessed day," turned into casual conversations and eventual relationships with these other women. Carol began ride-sharing with a couple of the girls. They would meet at a mutual location and take turns driving. Their conversations became more than casual. They would share their hearts with Carol, she would pray with them, and she had many opportunities to share her hope in Christ.

They would celebrate together when one of the husbands was released from prison. Carol lifted those up who were angry, discouraged, or depressed over their circumstances. She taught them how to love and honor their spouse, even in their dire situation. Over time, the faces of the commuters would change, but the message was always the same: God will never leave you nor forsake you! He loves you and has a plan for your life.

Dan had his own ministry. He was teaching Bible studies, utilizing his background in theology and his training in the PEACE Plan, an evangelical model for loving your neighbors, wherever you are. The men were so hungry for God's message. Dan was able to mentor individuals as well as speak to groups. One of his favorite things to do was to walk the track with the men. He would speak into an individual's life and heart, giving him hope for his future through Jesus.

When Dan got "in trouble" for sharing his faith, he was sent to a solitary cell. Satan did not like what was happening, and he was working to thwart the efforts. When he returned to his group living, Dan had to be creative. They would "play cards," while he continued to share the gospel with those who were willing to listen and receive the message. His walks became the heart-beat of his ministry with the men who were interested in continuing to grow.

God puts us in places where our hearts beat uniquely with others and we can walk by their side through adversity. It is Christ living through us, using us as His vessels, that brings hope and illuminates the knowledge and power of God.

Another area of Dan's expertise that God was able to use was his mechanical and engineering abilities. Taft Correctional Institution just happened to have a World for Wheels restoration shop, a ministry sponsored by Joni Eareckson Tada. Joni's organization sends used wheelchairs to prisons, where the wardens and supervisors monitor inmates who repair and restore broken and abused wheelchairs. These restored wheelchairs are sent back out into communities for those who need them.

Dan not only helped restore the basic wheel chairs, but he had the expertise to work on those chairs that needed mechanical attention. Through the work he did at the prison restoration shop over the decade plus he was serving his time, Dan repaired hundreds of wheelchairs. He was able to get the mechanical and electrical parts of the equipment up and running again. It was a blessing to others, and a blessing to him, to be able to work in this capacity during a time when he could have felt useless.

Toward the end of Dan's sentence, Carol was able to connect with a friend who lived in Glendora. Carol would drive up and stay with her friend on Saturday night, eating up about half of the distance she would need to travel to visit Dan the next day. Those connections were food for Carol's soul. Her friend loved, prayed, cried, and challenged Carol's faith. God knew that the encourager needed some encouragement, and He provided it at just the right time!

Twelve years is a long time, but it finally came to its conclusion. Dan was released. He seemed weaker than when he entered, in spite of having state-of-the-art gym equipment at the prison to stay in shape. His most immediate "job" when he began to assimilate back into society was to be a care giver for a dying friend. It was tough work, requiring lifting and moving the gentleman who could not move himself. Eventually they laid this friend to rest.

One of the joys of that time was the walks Carol and Dan were able to take along the beautiful coastal homes and views of the Pacific Ocean. God was giving them back some of the years the locusts had eaten. They reflected on how God had given them the hill country around Taft, and now He was using them and allowing them to enjoy the bluffs above the Pacific Ocean.

The reason for his weakened state became apparent when within three years, Dan was diagnosed and succumbed to pancreatic cancer. Carol had questions. Why would God heal Dan from the Myasthenia Gravis and allow him to live, just to go to prison? Now that he was out, why would God not heal him again from the cancer and restore him to greater ministry opportunities? In a devotional by Rick Warren, he stated that we don't need an explanation from God for our "whys." What we do need, God provides. We need strength. We need a Savior. We need comfort and support.

God was all those things to Carol and Dan. He taught them to live on **higher ground**, to trust Him for His goodness and perfect will in whatever circumstance they were living through. Shortly after Dan breathed his last breath, one of Carol's friends who had been praying for Dan, called. She said the Lord had made it clear to her that Dan had done everything God had wanted him to do. Now Jesus wanted Dan to be with Him.

So, what are your most fruitful life moments? It wouldn't surprise me if you were to answer that question with a story of your own pain and sorrow. It's in our seasons of total dependency when God builds our character and makes us into the person He created us to be. He takes our places of deepest despair and brings us to heights of hope, joy, and purpose. God will give us the hill country that He has promised.

Summing it Up:

- God's ways are higher and better than ours, and we can trust Him for that always! God has a plan for all of us based on His goodness, not on our greatness.
- Whether we're angry, discouraged, or depressed over our circumstances, God will never leave us nor forsake us.
- God puts us in places where our hearts beat uniquely with others and we can walk by their side through adversity. It is Christ living through us, using us as His vessels, that brings hope and illuminates the knowledge and power of God.
- It is just like Christ to use our weaknesses to show His strength.
- Sometimes the encourager needs encouragement, and God will provide it at just the right time.
- God will give back the years the locusts have eaten.
- We don't need an explanation from God for our "whys." What we do need, God provides. We need strength. We need a Savior. We need comfort and support.
- God does not fail in giving us our "hill country." We must be willing to accept it with the challenges it may present.

Highlights from God's Word:

- Isaiah 55:8-9

- Deuteronomy 31:8
- Psalm 138:8; 2 Corinthians 1:3-4
- 2 Corinthians 12:10
- 1 Thessalonians 5:11
- Joel 2:25-27
- Psalm 91:15
- Joshua 14:10-12

Memos of Mountaintop Moments

Journeys to Higher Ground

Chapter 11
SHELTERED BY THE MOST HIGH

He who dwells in the shelter of the Most High will rest in the shadow of the Almighty. Psalm 91:1

The annual trek to the Los Angeles Marathon was once again arriving. Preparation and gruesome training had been endured. The pledges for water had come in for Team World Vision, and Al was as ready as ever!

This was no ordinary feat. Al was not a twenty-, forty-, or even sixty-something youngster readying for the race. Al was seventy-three. It was March 2020, and this was his 4th Los Angeles Half-Marathon with the team from Bakersfield.

The anticipated moment came. The race started, and two hours, forty-eight minutes later, Al came successfully to the marathon's conclusion. His wife, Joyce, cheered for him as he crossed the finish line. They gathered their things and headed to the van for their transport back home.

Two weeks later, Joyce woke up with a really bad headache. That same day, Al began feeling exhausted and was having a hard time breathing. When his fever would not go down, they decided it was time to get Al to the hospital.

Al tested positive for Covid-19. This dreaded disease was just beginning to rear its ugly head in Kern County. Al was one of the first to be put on a ventilator in one of the local Bakersfield hospitals, and many of the treatments and methods were still on a trial basis.

Later, the questions began to come. How could someone so in shape be so sick? Why did Joyce, who also was diagnosed with Covid-19 and had underlying health concerns, recover so much sooner? Why did none of the other World Vision team members come down with it? These questions might never receive an answer, but one thing was for certain: Al's Covid journey was nothing short of a miracle.

His body had begun to shut down. He had already been on the ventilator well past the acceptable norm. Medications and the inability to rid his body of the toxins from the disease caused his kidneys to stop working. He required daily dialysis treatments, sometimes multiple times per day. He was in a coma, but the danger of moving him to get a brain MRI posed too great a risk.

His care proceeded without knowing if he had any brain activity. Several times Joyce had to answer the question of whether or not she wanted to take him off the ventilator. Her response was always the same, "If God wants him, He's going to have to come and get him." She was hanging onto hope, and she was leaning on the prayers of so many people from their church and community.

Joyce read Psalm 91 daily, sometimes multiple times in a day. She would put Al's name and circumstance in the passage, claiming and praying for his healing:

"He who dwells in the shelter of the Most High will rest in the shadow of the Almighty. I will say of the Lord, 'he is my fortress, my God, in whom I trust.' Surely he will save [Al] from the fowler's snare and from the deadly pestilence. He will cover [Al] with his feathers, and under his wings [Al] will find refuge; His faithfulness will be our shield and rampart..."

And so, it went, as Joyce repeated this passage, choosing to keep her trust on **higher ground**.

Though outwardly Al didn't seem to be responsive, he had his own moments of silent mental clarity. At one point he let God know he was ready to go. God gave him two very clear messages: 1) You are going to live; 2) You will have a story to share. Al kept fighting. Of course, no one knew he had this amazing encounter with God. They didn't even know if his brain was functioning. Then it happened.

Joyce was "talking" to him via facetime. In his comatose state, no one knew what Al was hearing or comprehending from these calls. When Joyce told Al she loved him, the nurses were excited to see that his heart rate increased. Later, his daughter jokingly told him that if he didn't get better, she was going to sell all of his tools. Again, his heart rate soared. Two of the earthly things that meant so much to Al were causing an increase on the heart monitor. Jesus' words from the sermon on the mount in the gospel of Matthew rang true. Where our treasure is, there our heart is also (see Matthew 6:21).

Easter Sunday was particularly tough on the family. The hospital called to tell them they needed to prepare to say their good-byes. Al's system was septic, and they could not seem to get the fluids to drain properly. They were losing him. That's when the prayers were amped up. People sat in the hospital parking lot in their cars and held a prayer vigil. It was totally up to God at this point.

The prayers of God's people were heard. Instead of Easter being the pivotal point for his life's final moments as the doctors assumed, it was the moment when things began to turn around. Shortly thereafter, the fluids began to drain. The initial medically-induced coma had been for five days. The following twenty-one days of Al's comatose state were finally coming to an end. His eyes began to open, just in a blank stare, but it was progress they had not seen prior to this moment.

The next six days were critical. His eyes went from being open, to blinking, to being able to move from side to side. The rest of his body was not moving, but he could now answer yes/no questions by blinking his eyes. After thirty-one days on the ventilator, the doctors determined it was time to remove it. If Al's breathing didn't resume naturally, they would not reintubate. Joyce was not allowed to watch as they took away this machine that had breathed for Al for many days. The staff watched closely as Al continued inhaling and exhaling on his own. Something so many of us take for granted was a true working miracle!

The doctor had told Joyce that Al would be confused when he came out of his coma. He would probably not know what was going on, and would not be very lucid. Wrong! The first time Al was able to talk with Joyce, he wanted to know if she had paid the bills and what the state of the pool was. He was able to remember the passwords to his on-line payment accounts, and he was able to give Joyce the instructions she needed to carry on at home.

On the second day of communicating, Al sang to Joyce with the sweet lyrics, "I just called to say I love you." When he was encouraged to sing to the nurse, Al knew he needed to change the tune. For this occasion, he pulled out another song from his memory bank. It was obvious that his humor had not left him when he crooned, "I just want to get out of this place."

Al was far from ready to be sent home, but such encouraging signs gave everyone hope. Rehabilitation began. He had to be taught to move his atrophied muscles. He had to relearn how to swallow so that he could start eating solid food. Prayers continued. Hospital staff came by the window to his room just to see him wave. They knew they were seeing a miracle, and they needed the hope his recovery symbolized as the pandemic continued to ratchet up.

The day came to move him from the ICU floor to a private room on another floor. He received excellent care. Therapy continued. They were preparing him for the moment where he could be relocated to a rehab center.

When the day came, people showed up in droves outside the rehab facility. They were awaiting the ambulance that was bringing Al from the hospital. As he was wheeled into the building, he smiled and waved at the crowd. The news was there to cover this miraculous event. The World Vision team of runners was there. Everyone cheered and clapped as we witnessed this dramatic event.

Two more weeks in rehab (a total of sixty-two days from the time he had first been admitted to the hospital) had Al standing on his own and walking with a walker. He ate as much as he could, according to the guidelines of the doctors, to try to gain some of the weight he had lost during the illness. Even with the extra intake of food, the day he left the rehab center, his clothes were barely hanging on him.

The next celebration was a drive-by while he and Joyce and other family members sat on their front lawn. Horns were honking, people were cheering and clapping, and tears were flowing as the line of vehicles serpentined down their street. They were amazed as they realized how many people had been supporting them in prayer through his ordeal.

Al continued gaining strength day-by-day, continuing his rehab at home. On a fall Sunday morning, when the congregation was having an outdoor service due to Covid restrictions, Al—minus his walker—and Joyce walked in. What praises and rejoicing we all felt.

Al and Joyce feel humbled that God chose to work in their lives in this miraculous way. They know this was not the case for everyone. They have their own story of losing their son to cancer. We could get so caught up or bogged down with the "whys." Why this person and not another? Why their son who was taken so young, and not Al or Joyce with their health issues?

While pondering the many why questions that seemed to keep coming into her mind, Joyce's conclusion was that "Why" is the Devil's question. He puts it in her mind to try to get her to doubt God and His sovereignty. This doesn't mean we should never ask why. The Psalms are full of David's "whys." The key is what we do with our whys. We probably won't get the answers we want while here on earth. However, we can come to the same conclusion shown over and over in King David's Psalms. "But I trust in your unfailing love; my heart rejoices in your salvation. I will sing to the Lord, for he has been good to me" (Psalm 13:5-6).

The Vaughns and their prayer support team that reached around the world called upon the Lord. He answered the prayers and delivered Al from death's door. Al is, of course, preparing for his next half-marathon in 2022. (As of the time of this writing, he is planning on a ten-mile training run tomorrow.) He'll probably be honored with a medal for a top time in his age group, but nothing compares to the honor God has bestowed upon him! (See Psalm 91:15)

Summing it Up:

- Psalm 91 is just one of many promises we can claim and pray, putting our own name or the name of a loved one in as we read or recite the passage.
- What we treasure on Earth is closely tied to our heart.
- The concerted prayers of God's people are powerful!
- Our "whys" become the Devil's tool if we allow him to use it to sow and cultivate doubt about God's goodness. David often asked why, but always came to the same conclusion: The Lord has been good to me.

Highlights from God's Word:

- Psalm 91
- Matthew 6:21

- Matthew 18:20
- Psalm 13:1-6

Memos of Mountaintop Moments

Chapter 12
GOD IS FOR YOU

What, then, shall we say in response to this? If God is for us, who can be against us? Romans 8:31

"You will not graduate from college. Your learning disability will impede you from furthering your education."

The words from Brad's science teacher reverberated in the room. Brad was completely deflated. He had hopes and dreams of becoming an ophthalmologist. Upon hearing this declaration, he knew his life and aspirations were over.

Seventh-grade Brad was sitting in a meeting with his parents, his teachers, and some administrators for his yearly Individualized Education Program (IEP) review. The teacher probably wasn't being vindictive. He most likely thought he was just stating a simple fact. But those words stuck with Brad through decades of his life. For Brad they were a sentence of failure and defeat. He already felt like he was the only one who had any problems with learning. He suffered from anxiety issues because of it. He knew he had to work harder than anyone else to achieve in school. He never wanted to speak in front of others because he was sure it would expose his weaknesses. He didn't need anyone to remind him of what he already knew.

Brad had known for some time that he was different from other kids when it came to learning. He was talented and friendly, athletic and musical, but reading, writing, spelling, and math came hard. He was embarrassed about it, and tried to compensate by appearing as if everything was fine. When he was tested in 5th grade, the psychologists and educators determined that he had an auditory processing disorder. Sounds and words became jumbled in his brain before he could make total sense of them. It created problems like stuttering, reading difficulties, and, ultimately, learning in most subject areas.

In spite of the looming prediction, Brad ended up enrolling in college. From the beginning, it was a struggle getting through the general education classes. He was failing his courses. He had pretty much decided that his seventh-grade science teacher's prophecy had come true. To Brad's relief, Point Loma professor, Dr. Jim Johnson, specializing in special education, came by his side. He provided the support and offered the strategies that Brad needed to get through his classes and eventually graduate.

His gratitude toward Dr. Johnson was beyond expression, but there was another event toward the end of Brad's junior year in college that changed his life! Brad traveled in a singing group that represented the college. On one particular weekend, their group came to his home town. After their concert, a dear saint in the church, Carol Unfried (who also happens to be my mother-in-law), felt led to pray over Brad, specifically about his learning disability.

A group of people gathered around Brad and prayed over him. An amazing thing happened. When Brad returned to school, he found himself more motivated. The strategies he had been implementing started making sense. His grades began to improve, and things that had previously been out of his control began to click. Brad knew that this monumental time in his life was a miracle of healing. It built his faith and increased his confidence level.

Brad graduated with his degree in education in 1999, and he and his wife moved to Arizona. He felt a true calling on his life to go into special education. He had been through so much himself, and he could relate to the pain that the students experienced. Going into this field would require furthering his degree. While working at a private day school called ACCEL (Arizona Centers for Comprehensive Education and Life Skills), Brad began a Master's program in Special Ed.

This was a guy who was not supposed to make it in higher education. The road was not easy. He first had to defend his GPA that had been affected by his Freshman and Sophomore grades at PLNU. Once getting through that hurdle, he effectively finished his course work in 2003. The only thing left was to take a comprehensive test to complete the Master's degree. Brad was terrified of any test, much less a cumulative one like this. He rationalized that he didn't really need the "paper" to declare his degree. He let his fear win for the moment. He continued working at the private school without obtaining the official title and diploma. He figured the knowledge base he had acquired through his studies would be sufficient for carrying on the work with his students.

Brad soon realized that his music background aided in teaching his special education students. Music helped facilitate language skills, improved attention spans, and served as motivation. When the special-education program seemed to need a boost, Brad worked with his administration to establish a music and literacy recording studio. Students were able to write and perform original pieces designed to inspire their creativity, foster self-dignity, and showcase their unique abilities. Over the course of several years, Brad and his students produced three albums.

The students learned money skills and social skills through the selling and promoting of the albums. They gained confidence and pride in a job well done. One particular student, who has severe autism, responded in an unexpected way. He typically became very anxious in small spaces. Yet, when he walked into the studio, the presence of a guitar and music helped create a non-threatening environment for him. This student loved "The Hokey Pokey." Brad and his team put that song on an album, and it became part of one of the many surprising success stories.

Brad received a phone call from the parents of this student shortly after Christmas. They related how their son would not come out for family gatherings around the holidays. The ten or so relatives who had come together for Christmas Day overwhelmed him, so he had opted to stay in his room. His parents decided to play the album with "The Hokey Pokey." When the song came on, they heard the door to their son's room open. He ran out to the living room and began singing and dancing uninhibitedly. The family members joined in the celebration and danced together for the best Christmas party they had ever experienced. With tears, these parents thanked Brad for helping their child to overcome some of his greatest fears.

Remember, Brad understood fear. We must also remember that the Lord knew Brad's fears, and He had plans to break through these fears and show Brad God's love and grace. In 2010, Brad was diagnosed with thyroid cancer. After an intense radiation treatment protocol, Brad had to be in isolation for a week. God used this quiet time to begin placing a call on Brad's heart to become a music minister. Brad was scared to death! Remember the part about not wanting to speak in front of people for fear of being exposed for who he was? Based on the pain of his past, he was sure he wasn't qualified to lead people.

God began a journey of redeeming the deepest places of his fear and insecurity. Brad benefited from another period of healing as he stepped into God's call on his life. In 2011 he became a bi-vocational music minister at his church. He was still working for ACCEL. In 2013 an opportunity arose for Brad to enter into an administrative role at the school. You guessed it! He needed to have a completed Master's degree!

Brad transitioned into a new role as a Mentor Teacher while he tried to figure out how he could finish what he had started over a decade ago. At this time Dr. Johnson came back into the picture. He was able to convince Chapman University, where Brad had completed his Master's coursework, to allow Brad to take the comprehensive test that he had previously avoided. God helped Brad, each step of the way. He was whispering into his ear, "You can do this! I am for you. I am with you." In 2018 Brad successfully completed the test and earned his Master's degree.

God worked in pivotal places in Brad's life. Through hardship, cancer, struggle, and pain, the Lord was getting Brad's attention. He brought him, ever so gently, to a place of intimacy that allowed for the deep spiritual healing that needed to take place. God continued to speak the words, "You are my child," and Brad began to truly accept God's view of him. He began to understand that God's plan for him was not just to advance his career, but to restore his wounded soul.

In 2019, Brad became the director of training and program development at ACCEL. How ironic that this new position required him to coach, mentor and train people in settings where he had to communicate to large groups. God continued to expand Brad's territory. Later that year, an energy and chemicals company from Saudi Arabia, called Saudi Aramco, approached Brad's team. This company had done their research globally to find an organization that would help them give back to their community in a specific way.

Saudi Aramco saw a need to build an infrastructure for helping students with disabilities in a country where there was no comprehensive program in place. When they discovered the prototype Brad had helped to develop at ACCEL in Phoenix, Arizona, though a comparatively small model, they knew it was what they were looking for. The motto "A life of dignity and self-worth," resonated with what the company was hoping to bring to their culture's negative view and treatment of some of the more severely disabled population.

In May of 2019, Brad and his team implemented their program in Saudi Arabia. They worked with families, assessed the needs, and facilitated the start-up of appropriate educational programs. One apprehensive Saudi mother snuck upstairs without checking in at the school's front desk. She had a great distrust that anyone could truly help her son. She wanted to hear what was being taught and how her son was being treated.

Brad was tasked to search this mom out and speak with her. When he caught up with her, they began walking down the hall together. He pointed out what they were hoping to do for her eleven-year-old quadriplegic son. Though she was wearing a burqa that exposed only her eyes, Brad could tell she was crying. She pointed to the sign with the motto, and said, "Today is the first day of my son's life!" Decades earlier, in a routine IEP meeting, Brad had felt like his life had been over. God had redeemed that moment, and now Brad was being used to bring hope and life to others across the globe.

Our words are so important. They can bring such healing and life to someone, or they can crush their spirit. Pray that God will use your words for good!

Maybe you are a recipient of crushing words. There is healing for you! God is the lifter of your head! He understands your fears and your insecurities, and He wants to be your strength. He has made you unique. God can use your special gifts, and even your experiences (positive and negative), to help others and broaden your sphere of influence in ways you would never have imagined.

Listen to God's voice that tells you that you are His child, not the inner voice of condemnation and shame. He has plans to prosper you, not to harm you. Remember that you have the God of the Universe on your side. He can lead you to a place of **higher ground**. Lean into Him, as Brad learned to do, and let Him use your story of redemption to bring hope and life to others.

Summing it Up:

- Our words are so important. They can bring such healing and life to someone, or they can crush their spirit.
- There is healing for you! God is the lifter of your head!
- God has made you in a unique and wonderful way.

- God can use your special gifts, and even your experiences (positive and negative), to help others and broaden your sphere of influence in ways you wouldn't even have imagined.
- You are God's precious child.
- God has amazing plans for your life!
- Remember that you have the God of the Universe on your side.

☀ Highlights from God's Word:

- Proverbs 16:24; Proverbs 15:4
- Psalm 3:3; Psalm 146:8
- Psalm 139:13-16
- 1 Chronicles 4:9-10
- Galatians 3:26
- Jeremiah 29:11
- Romans 8:31

Memos of Mountaintop Moments

Chapter 13
GOD'S HAND

Moses answered the people, "Do not be afraid. Stand firm and you will see the deliverance the Lord will bring you today."
Exodus 14:13a

Kirk Allen lives by faith and by the belief that even when we don't see it at the moment, God's hand is working every single day in our lives. We just have to be looking for it. This was especially evident when God parted the "Red Sea" for the Allens before, during, and after Kirk's heart attack.

To give a little background on Kirk and Annette, his wife, they lived and worked full time at Hume Lake Christian Camps in the Sierra Nevadas from 2000-2013. If you want to talk about **higher ground,** this would be the place. Located at 5200 feet, this camp ministers to kids, teens and adults throughout the year through camps, retreats, and seminars. They have amazing activities and opportunities for fun, but their mission is clear: bring people to a saving, growing faith in Christ, and help them to establish discipleship habits that they can take back home with them. The setting is gorgeous, the atmosphere is stellar, and the result is that you leave better than when you came.

Kirk worked as the Maintenance Supervisor for the camp. Due to constant training of the temporary summer staff, the immensity of the campus and its projects, and Kirk's strong work ethic, this job carried with it a lot of stress. It came with the territory, and Kirk accepted it in stride (or so he thought).

In 2008 and 2009, Kirk had noticed that he felt tired all the time. Other than that, he felt pretty good, but his energy level was not what he was used to. He chalked it up to getting older, the altitude, and the constant demands on him, physically and emotionally.

In July of 2009 Kirk was taking his summer staff down the hill to Visalia for a little fun, some bonding, and a break from the routine. After about a two-hour trip down the mountain, the group arrived at a go-kart venue to unwind. Kirk was in the middle of a race with a few of his staff, when he noticed a tightening in his chest. He was determined to finish the race, so he ignored the symptoms and put the pedal to the metal. It was a hot central valley evening, and when he came to a stop, besides the fact that he had lost the race, he noticed that he was profusely sweating.

Still not overly concerned, Kirk hydrated and tried to settle his body down. Having had former EMT training and experience, Kirk began to realize this was not normal. His daughter, Brittany, who was with the group, was commissioned to take him to the Kaweah-Delta Hospital that was just minutes away. As they were driving toward the health center, Kirk told Brittany she better call her mom, Annette, who had stayed up at Hume to finish her work week.

Upon entering the hospital, the front desk clerk was having Kirk fill out paperwork. He finally looked at the employee and said, "We can fill this stuff out later. I need to have someone take a look at me." Minutes later, he was taken back for an EKG. It didn't take long for the staff to realize what was happening. Suddenly, there were about twelve hospital workers surrounding him, removing his clothes, and putting nitro under his tongue.

Kirk was put on a gurney to be taken to the "cath" lab for cardiac catheterization. They told him he was going to be fine, but that he was having a heart attack. One of the nurses explained to Kirk that the on-call physician, Dr. Sharma, was one of the best. While some doctors unwind by going to the golf course, Dr. Sharma unwinds by spending time in this lab. He designed it; it was his baby. Kirk doesn't remember much after that, except for the dye being shot into his veins. He eventually had a stent put in due to complete blockage of the main artery to his heart. This kind of blockage only has a five percent recovery rate. It wasn't until seeing the before and after pictures later that he could actually see the state of his cardiovascular system. The flow of blood could be seen to a particular point, and then it just stopped. After the stent was inserted, the "river" with its thousands of tributaries was once again functioning and streaming through as normal.

In the meantime, a social worker had been assigned to Brittany since she was alone. She calmly explained what was happening and gave Brittany the support she needed. The social worker sat with her until Annette arrived. Annette had received the call from Brittany while she was at home, resting from the day, having just given blood at the Hume Lake mobile blood drive. She thought it was pretty weird that Kirk was at the hospital because he just never gets sick. She felt compelled to grab a bag with some of her things, even though the information in the call was that Kirk was at the hospital, but he was going to be okay.

It was already becoming dark as Annette began the trip down the hill to Visalia. On a Saturday shopping day, it would usually take her about two hours to get down the mountain. This evening it took her a mere hour and fifteen minutes. As she recalled the events, she admitted to going a little fast, but the miracle was that there was not a single car on the road before or behind her the entire way. God was parting the "Red Sea."

Kirk stayed in the hospital for seven days. He was thoroughly examined and released to go back to Hume, on limited work responsibility. The doctor determined that Kirk was actually in good health. His cholesterol looked fine. His strength and weight, eating habits, and exercise regimen were good. Nothing really needed to be changed. "Keep up the good work," the doctor admonished, "EXCEPT reduce your stress."

Our bodies can be in excellent physical condition, but when we do not allow ourselves to properly rest and reboot throughout the day, we are setting ourselves up for potential disaster. Certain amounts of stress can be helpful in motivating us to accomplish tasks, meet deadlines, and fulfill obligations. But chronic stress related to extreme ongoing issues must be curbed. It takes intentional life-style changes like making and taking time for fun, renewing and strengthening our minds through God's Word, and examining the tasks set before us in a new light.

Kirk and Annette are so grateful for the second chance they got to live out God's purpose in their lives. They continued to see His hand parting the way throughout this experience and ultimate decisions and changes in careers and location. Besides the road to Visalia being cleared before Annette, there were a couple of other significant Red Sea events that showed God's hand.

Just the fact that they were in Visalia, not Hume Lake, close to a hospital and able to get treatment quickly, was a miracle. A few days earlier, Kirk and Annette and a few others had gone four-wheeling in the backcountry. They spent several days hiking, exploring, and enjoying God's beautiful creation. If Kirk's heart-attack had occurred during this trip, results could have been quite different. Not only were they a couple hours from a hospital, they were a couple of additional hours from civilization. There was no cell phone service, no easy way to drive out of the wilderness, and no quick access to any medicines or treatments that he would have needed.

The heart attack also got them thinking about their future. It put Kirk on a track to get his Wastewater Operation Certificate. Over the course of the next three years, God led him through on-line schooling, certification, and eventual licensing. He needed 1800 hours of on-the-job experience before he could be licensed. He applied with six hundred other applicants for a job in Tulare. When it seemed impossible, God parted the waters once again. Kirk was eventually called back for a series of tests, panel interviews, and final interviews (from 600 applicants down to three). He got the job and was able to finish the process. God continued surprising and parting the way as He used Kirk to speak into the life of his supervisor, who desperately needed to hear a word from God through a willing servant.

As the time came for the Allens to consider where they might want to settle into retirement years, they went on a location search up and down California. They loved the Redding area, where there was a wastewater plant, but no job availability. Within a few weeks, a flier came across Kirk's desk regarding an opening in the City of Shasta Lake. He applied, got the job, and relocated shortly thereafter. God's hand was once again parting the way.

We tend to think that the Red Sea parting was THE major event for showing God's glory in the Israelites relocation from Egypt to

Canaan. It definitely was that, but even now God continues to part the way to show His glory in our daily lives. It's important to look for Him, and recognize the moving of His hand as He creates miraculous paths for us to walk through.

Summing It Up:
- God's hand is working every day in our lives.
- The "Red Seas" of our lives can be parted in miraculous ways.
- Stress can be good, however, too much stress can be harmful. We need to learn to rest and be still.
- God has multi-purposes for our lives and wants to use you right where you are.
- God's desire is to bring glory to Himself through our lives and circumstances.

Highlights from God's Word:
- Job 12:10; Romans 8:28
- Exodus 14:13; Hebrews 11:29
- Psalm 46:10
- 1 Peter 4:10-11
- Isaiah 43:6-7

Memos of Mountaintop Moments

Chapter 14
WHERE AND HOW?

*I lift up my eyes to the hills—where does my help come from?
My help comes from the Lord, the Maker of heaven
and earth. Psalm 121:1-2*

Have you ever found yourself asking, "Lord, WHERE are you?" or "Lord, HOW am I going to get through this?" These questions usually swirl through your brain when you are in the middle of a crisis that seems unsolvable. You feel like you have exhausted all your human resources. You are at rock bottom—spiritually, emotionally, physically, financially, or maybe you're experiencing a combination of these.

It is during these times when the only direction you can look is up. In order to rise above your circumstances, to get to **higher ground**, you have to look to the One from whom your help comes. It comes from the Lord. He is the Maker of heaven and earth. He does not slumber nor sleep. Psalm 121 gives such hope. You can be assured that:

- He will help and protect you
- He will keep you from harm
- He will watch over your life

We are given Biblical examples of this. Joseph, as a young teen, looked up from the bottom of a pit when he was sold into Egyptian slavery by his brothers. Later Joseph gazed up from a prison cell where he had been unjustly placed. Through trusting the Maker of heaven and earth, Joseph eventually rose to a place of leadership, second only to the reigning Pharaoh. God watched over him and kept his life from harm. More than that, God used the pain of his situation to bring about the saving of many lives (including those brothers who had originally intended to harm him).

Another example the Bible gives us is the life of Job. He had everything taken from him. His health was failing him, his family was gone, his wealth was but a memory, and his friends berated him. There was nowhere else to look but to God. God spoke to Job of His power and sovereignty. Job not only heard, but his eyes saw that God's plan for life sometimes included suffering. Job accepted his limited understanding of God's greatness, and he recognized God's love.

Laura Kirkemo relates to these two Biblical characters. Her life, as she describes it, was going pretty well. She had a good job, a good apartment, good friends, and a good church. In 2011, her dad passed away. A few months later her cat died, one that had been her companion for years. While she was grieving these two losses, she was grappling with the reality that she would need to become her mom's full-time caregiver. Her mom had been living with a diagnosis of Multiple Sclerosis (MS) for twenty-five years. With her dad gone, Laura would need to move into her parents' home and help her mom.

With her furniture in storage and a drastically altered life-style, Laura poured herself into her new role. She read books on God's miraculous power, and believed that her mom would be healed. She decided that it must be a lack of her mom's faith or a sin problem that she needed to deal with since the healing didn't occur. It wasn't until her own illnesses that Laura looked back on the fallacy of this thinking and guilt-casting. Part of Laura's healing came as she confessed her own pride and sought her mom's forgiveness.

In 2015, Laura was diagnosed with pleurisy, a lung infection which took about eight months to heal. In 2016, she was hospitalized with Valley Fever. Ten days in the hospital and two months of carrying around an oxygen tank was just part of the road to recovery. Almost a year later, Laura noticed a large mass in her stomach. She returned to the same hospital as the previous year with a sweet friend who accompanied her to the appointment. When they were escorted into the room to hear the prognosis, Laura could tell by the faces of the doctors that the news was not good.

She was informed that she had Lymphoma. Her initial reaction was, "Of course, I do. Why not? What next?" She recognized that Satan was attacking her, throwing one sickness after another at her. As with Job's wife, there were those around her who probably thought she should curse God and die (Job 2:9). Instead, rather than getting bitter or questioning God, Laura grew deeper in her walk with Him. Through rounds of chemo, multiple doctor's visits, blood draws, and consultations, Laura dug deep into God's Word. She learned of the character of God, and He was able to soften her heart. Though God did not give her the cancer, she saw how He was working through it to give her great compassion and love for others.

After a short period of remission, the cancer returned. Her doctors advised that Laura be aggressive in her treatment of the now stage 4 cancer. After a couple of consulting appointments and listening to the Spirit of God speaking into her depths, she decided against continuing any further chemo. The effects it had on her body was causing such destruction that she chose to move forward without it.

Laura and her mom made another crucial, God-led decision. After her mom had been hospitalized due to some complications with MS, they prayed about whether or not to have her continue temporary care in a rehab facility or to come home. Their decision to have her come home came shortly before the coronavirus hit full force in the state of California. Had she been housed in the care facility, Laura would not have been able to visit or care for her mom. Instead, they were able to enjoy fellowship and care that would not have been possible otherwise.

It has not been an easy road. Most days Laura is exhausted. Besides hospice coming in for an hour or so each day, the bulk of responsibility lies with Laura. By necessity, she has become nurse, cook, shopper, and cleaner. She is taking care of the house maintenance and doing all the heavy lifting. There are days when she wonders if she can handle much more. With all her efforts going into her mom's care, Laura has not had much time to think about her cancer. Each day she recognizes the strength God is pouring over her.

Laura reminds herself often that God has promised to be her husband, counselor, advisor, doctor, and her salvation—her everything. She sees God's provision everywhere. Though this is not the life she would have hoped for or planned, she relies on her gracious God.

When Laura tries to figure things out, God gently reminds her, "You can't know my mind. I'm God, you're not! You don't need to be my Holy Spirit." She says, "I don't have to know why I haven't been healed of cancer, but I know this: He loves me. Everything He does is out of compassion and love for us." What a statement of faith! What a way to rise above circumstances.

Laura firmly believes that suffering is part of our story, our growth. When we have an intimate relationship with our Savior, we can look back and see that nothing in our lives was wasted. We are purified and refined through the fire and come out as gold.

In June of 2019, Laura was recognized by a group called H.O.W., which stands for Helping One Woman at a time. They receive nominations of women who are dealing with tough things in their lives. They honor them at a dinner and offer a monetary gift that is designed to help them with some of their expenses. Laura was asked to write her story for their newsletter. Her desire was that Christ would be glorified. She ended her "testimony" with this:

"I do not know what my future holds, but I do know my God has it all mapped out and it is good! I know that this cancer is a curse and Jesus took that curse for me on the cross. And by His shed blood, His finished work on the cross, I am set free from the curse of cancer. My physicians have told me I have 2-6 months to live, but I do not care what anyone says because the one true physician, Jehovah Rapha, has the final Word. The Spirit of God has made me; the breath of the Almighty gives me life (Job 33:4). He rejoices over me with singing (Zeph. 3:17). So if the Son sets me free, I am free indeed (John 8:36)."

Your story might not be as dramatic as Joseph's, Job's, or Laura's. It might be worse than all three. The same God who helped these three to rise above and come to a place of **higher ground** is the God you can rely on to help you through your circumstances.

Summing It Up:

- When you are in the middle of a crisis that seems unsolvable, you feel like you have exhausted all your human resources, and you are at rock bottom—spiritually, emotionally, physically, and/or financially—the direction to look is up. God is watching over your life.
- God used Joseph's trials to bring about His purpose.
- Job not only heard, but his eyes saw that God's plan for life sometimes included suffering. Job accepted his limited understanding of God's greatness, and he recognized God's love.
- When we have an intimate relationship with our Savior, we can look back and see that nothing in our lives was wasted. We are purified and refined through the fire and come out as gold.
- The Spirit of God has made me; the breath of the Almighty gives me life.
- He rejoices over me with singing.
- if the Son sets me free, I am free indeed.

Highlights from God's Word:

- Psalm 121
- Genesis 45:4-7
- Job 42:2-5
- 1 Peter 1:7
- Job 33:4
- Zephaniah 3:17
- John 8:36

Memos of Mountaintop Moments

Chapter 15
THE SWEET TASTE OF JOY

"My food," said Jesus, "is to do the will of him who sent me and to finish his work." John 4:34

When I get really busy and productive, I forget to eat. I don't even notice my hunger. My focus is my task, and I don't even feel hungry. It would be nice to have that problem all the time, but eventually someone in my family gets hungry, I stop to feed them, and the aromas and taste of the food overwhelm me. Whether I get a quick bite or sit down for a meal, I enjoy the nourishment and get back to work.

It has been two years since Richard has been able to smell or taste food. What would probably do most of us in, has brought Richard only a few brief days of depression. For the most part, he has accepted it as a part of the struggle he has faced. The surprising replacement for the lack of aromas and flavors has been the sweet taste of joy he has experienced over the past two years. He often jokes with his family, asking them if the food they're eating together really tastes as good as he remembers. They tease him with their "oohs" and "aahs." He gets back at them when they are complaining about the skunk on the road or the bad garbage with, "What are you talking about? I don't smell anything."

As I listened to Richard's recounting of his cancer journey, I kept thinking of Jesus' reply to his disciples when they were trying to get him to eat something. They had just come back from wherever they had been to find Jesus speaking with a Samaritan woman. In the culture of that day, Jews despised the Samaritans, and did not associate with them. Religious teachers rarely spoke with women in public. It's not hard to imagine how they tried to hide their surprise that Jesus was defying both of these cultural norms. As a distraction, they urged Jesus to eat something. Jesus had just spoken life into someone who desperately needed him. He truly was not concerned with eating physical food. He answered them, "My food is to do the will of him who sent me and to finish his work" (John 4:34).

Richard would love to taste food again, but most of the time he forgets about it as he is doing the work of his Heavenly Father. It all began in May, 2019, when he noticed a kink in his neck. Thinking he had just slept on it wrong, he reached up to touch it. He felt a searing pain and the affected area was hot. He decided to make a doctor's appointment, but he couldn't get in for a month. In the meantime, he called every day and checked on cancellations. A couple of weeks later his doctor's office was able to fit him into see a practitioner. By now the area was very swollen, looking like that of a buff football player whose neck has become one with his head.

The practitioner didn't seem too concerned. She checked his ears, gave him an antibiotic and sent him home. Fortunately, Richard had not canceled the original appointment with his doctor. Though the swelling had gone down, the lump remained. His regular doctor was livid that more attention had not been given to Richard's health issue. He scheduled him for an immediate CT scan. Richard was surprised to get a call back from the doctor on the same evening as the scan, a Saturday night no less. The lump was indeed cancer. It had originated in his tonsils and they would need to schedule a tonsillectomy and a biopsy as soon as possible.

By the end of June both procedures had occurred. Richard laughed at the fact that he had his tonsils out at age 60. During the biopsy, the concern was that the mass was behind his jugular vein, which could easily be nicked. Richard went into the procedure not too concerned about himself. His attitude was, if he had to suffer for a while and God healed him, he would praise the Lord. If he was to suffer for a while and God took him home, he would praise the Lord.

Since he wasn't under sedation for the process, he spoke to the nurses, doctors, technician, and ultrasound specialist letting them know he would be praying for them throughout the procedure. The reactions varied from surprise, to rejection, to thanks. None of that stopped him. He prayed out loud for the doctor's hands to work with precision, and that God would bless his hands when he worked on other patients as well.

Throughout all the prep work, including some dental procedures, Richard prayed that he could bring joy to those with whom he came into contact. At times he lifted the staff's spirits, as well as other patients who could hear what was going on, with jokes and lighthearted talk. At other times, Richard would ask them how he could pray for them. God was truly using him.

Things were moving quickly. By August 13, Richard moved to Hollywood, a couple of blocks from the main Kaiser facility there. He stayed in an apartment throughout the week so that he would be available for seven weeks of radiation and chemo treatments. His close proximity would make it possible for the medical team to take expedient action if there was a need for any further tests or probes. Richard and his wife, Tiffany, drove down to his apartment. He took stock of the furnishings, and soon declared the dining room table as his "war room." His Bible, journal, prayer request lists (which kept getting longer by the day), cards of encouragement, and schedules stayed on that table throughout the stay.

The first day of chemo and radiation came. The doctor was blunt about the expectations, not sugar coating anything. Richard assured the doctor that he did not need to wear Richard's burden. He was at peace with however God chose to work. Then he asked if it was permissible for him to talk with the other patients awaiting their treatments. Even though the rules wouldn't allow him to speak with the other chemo recipients, Richard knew he could still pray. He quickly realized that while waiting with the twenty or so individuals in the room, there were a lot of trips to the bathroom. They filled him with fluid to counteract some of the chemo effects. Each time he got up from his seat to use the facilities, he would go a different route. To each person he passed, he would say simply, "I'm praying for you." No one objected. He was technically not breaking the rules. And pray he did!

Back at his war room table, Richard was reading the book of John. The message Richard kept hearing from John was to go. This command manifested itself in a variety of ways. It was important for Richard to keep his body moving and not allow fatigue and listlessness to set in. He asked the Lord how he could serve. Each day he would walk five miles, a continuation of what he had been doing pre-cancer. Sometimes the walking was broken up between a morning and afternoon stint. And, yes, he prayed as he walked. He stopped and talked with homeless people, seeking to know their story. He poured out love and prayers on them. He continued to "go."

He also began to use his limited resources. He bought a few groceries for a family. He bought some items of clothing for a man who only owned one shirt and one pair of pants. People from the church began helping him with a few financial gifts to help where needed. One evening he found a $20 bill on the ground. He looked around, prayed, and made a bee-line for a gentleman who was sitting on a barrel talking to those around him. Richard gave it to him to be used for buying food. With a liquor store nearby, he wasn't sure what would happen, but when he made his way back toward his apartment, he saw the gentleman coming out of a store with two grocery bags. As Richard watched, the man handed the bags to two of the men he had been talking to. Richard was amazed at his generosity. He approached him and gave him another $20 from his own wallet, and told him to use it for himself. The man later told him he was able to eat for over a week on that gift.

On another day, Richard approached a couple who wanted to talk to him about a wildlife foundation they were involved in. He said he would listen to their spiel if they would listen to him at the end. When they finished, he agreed to give a small monthly donation. Then he talked to them about the Lord. He found out their stories, prayed for them, and blessed them. They were sobbing by the time it was done.

There are too many stories to tell, but of great interest was the Scientology building that was not too far from the hospital. People were constantly proselytizing as people passed by. Richard "rescued" a woman who was backed into a corner by calling her "mom" and asking her if she was ready to go. She looked at him without blinking an eye and said she was. Richard looked at those talking to her and asked why they didn't share about Jesus Christ. They immediately left and sent security to keep an eye on him.

Whenever he came around, he would always mention the name of Jesus. Most of the time the Scientologists would turn tail and leave him be. At the name of Jesus demons will flee!

The highlight of Richard's week was stopping by Olive Knolls Christian School, which was part of his work assignments, on Friday afternoons when he arrived back in Bakersfield. The students would crowd around him and let him know they were praying for him. He received a couple of prayer blankets from the fifth graders and the Celebrate Recovery participants. He believed that their prayers were getting him through and making a huge difference.

A big problem was eating. Because Richard had no smell or taste, he really had no desire to eat. If he lost more than 10% of his weight, they would have to put in a feeding tube. At first the lost pounds were welcomed, but when he saw that he was getting close to the endangered weight, he began to get creative. First, he would pray over every bite. "Lord, let me take this bite." He would get through a meal in this manner. He would find something he could eat, like oatmeal. It would work for a few days, then he would have to find a different food item. They weighed him every day during treatments. He began to carry water bottles in his pockets to add a few extra ounces to the scales. As weight continued to drop, he exchanged some money for rolls of quarters. He would weigh in with the quarters in his pockets helping him not go below the desired pounds.

After Labor Day, Richard and Tiffany were heading back to the apartment after a 3-day weekend. They had just taken the exit to the street leading to his humble abode when he realized he had left the keys back in Bakersfield. His daughter confirmed that they were at home, so they began the trek back. In the meantime, they stopped for a bite to eat at a McDonalds. As Richard was waiting in line to order food, God spoke to him to go talk to a young couple. The man was full of tattoos and was most certainly part of a gang. The security guards were eyeing the couple, making sure there wouldn't be trouble.

Richard argued with God for a minute, but as always was obedient. Richard meandered to their table and asked how they were doing. He ended up sitting with them, finding out why the man had entered gang life, and ministering God's love to both of them without judgment. The gang member's girlfriend was the daughter of a pastor. She knew of God's love and was concerned about her boyfriend. As they bowed in prayer in the McDonalds, the gang member grabbed Richard's hand. At the end of the prayer, they were all crying. Richard promised to continue praying for them.

As we were talking, I had to keep reminding myself that we were here because of Richard's cancer story. His selfless living was so impressive and convicting. Someone who could not taste much more than cinnamon, honeydew melon, and vanilla protein shakes; someone who had been through a grueling regimen of chemo and radiation; the one who should be complaining or at least requesting prayer for himself; this one was praying, loving, and serving others. Richard's joy was evident. It was disappointing to him, and a little depressing at times, to know that his taste and smell had not returned (and probably never will without God's intervention). He might not ever truly enjoy earthly food in the same way as the rest of us do, but he lives on **higher ground,** content with feeding on the will of the One who sent him.

Summing it Up:

- We would do well to follow the example of Jesus whose priority was doing the work of His Heavenly Father.
- Richard's attitude was if he was to suffer for a while and God healed him, he would praise the Lord. If he was to suffer for a while and God took him home, he would praise the Lord.
- Richard prayed as he walked. He stopped and talked with homeless people, seeking to know their story. He poured out love and prayers on them.
- Richard would always mention the name of Jesus. Those in opposition would turn tail and leave him be. At the name of Jesus demons will flee!

Highlights from God's Word:

- John 4:34
- Habakkuk 3:17-18
- Ephesians 6:18
- James 2:19 & 4:7

Memos of Mountaintop Moments

Chapter 16
A WORK IN PROGRESS

Be diligent in these matters; give yourself wholly to them, so that everyone may see your progress. 1 Timothy 4:15

In 1992 our church moved into our new facility. It was a plan that began in the mind and heart of the pastor at that time, Pastor Bert Rhodes. His vision was shared and developed by laymen and laywomen in the church. Church members gave and sacrificed time and resources to make it happen. We watched the progress until the day we moved in and dedicated the building fully to the Lord. Over time, improvements continued to be made. In recent days, repairs, repainting, and remodeling has taken place in order to keep the facility welcoming and functional. It is a work in progress, and continues to need care and change to remain a vital place where ministry can take place.

There was another work in progress which the congregation was watching, that of a miracle we had prayed for the year before. Our friends, Theresa and Mark West, had brought their 8-week-old daughter, Markli, with them to church, as was their family habit and routine. The Sunday Sermon by Pastor Mel Rich was about the four friends who had lowered a paralyzed man through the roof to be healed by Jesus. With that same faith, the Wests brought Markli, who had been diagnosed with cortical blindness, forward at the end of the service to pray for her healing. They were immediately surrounded by a surge of friends, people who were more like family. When you belong to a caring body of believers, the connecting bonds of love are powerful. It was in this environment that God chose to touch their daughter's sight.

Theresa grappled with her faith. She asked questions like, "How does God choose who he is going to heal?" He chose not to heal Deanne, another church member we had been praying for, from her cancer. He hadn't saved Theresa's sister in their growing up days from dying of leukemia before the age of five. Who were they to expect an answer from God for their little one? Yet she knew God could and would do it. It took a couple of years to experience all God had planned for them and Markli. Her story was definitely a work in progress.

Leading up to this moment, we must look back on Theresa's pregnancy. Mark and Theresa were called by their doctor in the second trimester of the pregnancy to have an amniocentesis due to an abnormal alpha-fetoprotein count. Too much or too little of this protein, produced in the liver of a developing fetus, can be an indicator of a possible birth defect, including genetic disorders or chromosomal abnormalities, such as Down syndrome. As it turned out, the doctor determined that the irregular levels had been caused by a miscalculation of the baby's due date.

Feeling greatly relieved, but also a little frustrated for having gone through such an invasive and potentially risky procedure, the Wests could now focus on their new little one. On July 11, 1991, Markli West was born.

From day one, Markli's little eyes were turning in. This is known as bilateral esotropia, a form of strabismus where one or both eyes turn inward. The pediatrician was concerned that she was actually blind. By eight weeks, she couldn't focus on objects. She wasn't smiling at people. This doctor was even more adamant that she most likely had little or no sight.

At about ten weeks old, Markli went in for an exam to check for optic nerve development. Since she would cry and squint her eyes when they needed to be able to dilate her pupils, she had to be put under anesthesia. The exam revealed that her optic nerves were one-third the size of normal. Optic nerves develop to their maturity during the first trimester of pregnancy, so there was no chance that would change. The pediatrician also told the Wests that most of the children who are born with this type of optic nerve hypoplasia also had severe mental retardation.

Another test, called the Visual Evoked Potential (VEP) test, was administered to determine if her optic nerves were receiving light. Electrodes were attached to her tiny head as visual stimuli from a computer screen displayed different patterns and contrasts to elicit the electrical response from the retina. The electrical energy was then sent to the visual cortex and recorded. Fortunately, their precious little bundle slept through this procedure. The test revealed that she was receiving light, but one eye was catching it slower than the other.

This was great news, but the experts still felt that as Markli grew older, she would only see a few inches in front of her face. Therefore, they connected the Wests with nurses who would order large-print books for her as she approached kindergarten. Theresa began to try to fathom the fact that her little girl would not be able to see Christmas lights or the details on the faces of her three older siblings. The parents contemplated learning Braille as a way to help their daughter. All of these thoughts felt overwhelming and hopeless.

The nurses also gave the Wests the contact information of other families with blind children. Theresa and Markli were visiting one particular home just as Markli was in the beginning stages of crawling. The mom of the three-year-old blind son observed, "I don't think your daughter is blind." She could see things in Markli that she hadn't seen in her own son.

At ten months, the doctor decided they should do surgery to correct the strabismus, purely for cosmetic reasons. With her eye muscles not working properly, the surgery would put them into proper alignment. Once again, they had to make the difficult decision of putting their daughter under the knife. Of course, they weighed the pros and cons, knowing that there were risks, as with all surgeries. The surgeon would incise a thin layer of transparent tissue which covers the eye muscles, in order to access these very thin muscles. The muscle edge was clipped to stretch and create the proper alignment of the eyes relative to each other. The procedure was successful and eventually, with the continued aid of prism lenses, the muscles were trained to respond properly, correcting the eye crossing.

Not too long after the surgery, Theresa recalled being in the mountains. They rounded a bend where a waterfall could be seen from a distance. Markli, who apparently had nothing wrong with her brain, despite what the doctor had warned, was already talking up a storm as she approached her first-year birthday. She declared, "My daddy made that." Was she seeing it, or just hearing it? Clearly, she knew her daddy could do just about anything. He was her hero, but Theresa pondered these things in her heart. She believed that Markli and her Heavenly Daddy had made some special connections in the early days of her sight challenges. The same good Father who created the waterfalls and the mountains had healed her blindness.

The pediatric ophthalmologist shot straight with them. He let them know she would have impaired depth perception. They still didn't know the extent to which she was blind, because she couldn't tell them, in spite of her increasing vocabulary, so they continued watching for other signs. The doctor would lay out quarters in the hallway when they visited just to see if she could find them. That was a piece-of-cake for Markli. She would go right for the quarters, pick them up, and put them in her mouth.

As Markli was approaching two, her speech was developing rapidly. Her ophthalmologist told Theresa she had trained Markli to act like a sighted child. Taken aback by this, Theresa decided to bring in a picture book one day. Going out of order to make sure Markli hadn't just memorized the order of the pictures, and having the doctor hold it several feet away, Markli began identifying the pages. "Hippopotamus. Circle. Giraffe." The doctor began to study Markli's chart, as if he was trying to make sure this was the same child he was thinking about.

In the meantime, they canceled her large-print books. At about nineteen months, the doctor signed off on her charts, releasing her from the need for future monitoring. Theresa had kept the observation notes from the doctors along the way, documenting the suspense and fearfulness of the process they had gone through. As far as they could tell, the healing was a process over time. The special healing prayer was just the beginning. Through the surgeries, tests, and treatments, plus Markli's development as she grew from infancy to toddler, God was doing His healing work.

Mark commented that he never doubted that everything would be fine in the long-run, but never would have scripted it in the way it turned out. His perspective of miracles changed. We tend to want to see the miracle happen right now, instantaneously, like when Jesus would heal. Instead, there was a waiting period. The miracle was not just the end result, but it happened as part of their journey. As a pastor, Mark has brought that perspective into his discipleship training. We don't necessarily instantaneously arrive to the place God has in store for us. It is a process, a series of phases. It's part of our faith walk.

From the point of healing prayer to her release by the ophthalmologist, it was a progressive healing. There were little milestones along the way that were aided by surgery, prism lens glasses (after surgery), and the improvements that were being charted and seen with each appointment. The skepticism of the doctor as he saw how far Markli had come along was clearly being disputed by the evidence. It gave Mark and Theresa the opportunity to share their faith and their belief that God had healed her.

Today, Markli wears corrective lenses for far-sightedness. She can see fine at a distance, but she has to wear glasses or contacts for close-up vision and reading. The only thing the doctors felt like she would never be able to do was to fly a plane because of the peripheral and depth perception issues. What a far cry from the original diagnosis of cortical blindness. Pilot or not, the Wests knew God had lifted her to **higher ground** through her healing.

There are many types of blindness in this life. At some point we are blind to our sin. We feel justified in doing what we want, when we want. We are blind to God's goodness. How can a good God let bad things happen? We are blind to our need for Him. We are told over and over by the world that if we just try hard enough and believe in ourselves, we can accomplish anything. God progressively, over time, reveals Himself to us. He opens our eyes to who He is and what we can become in Him. We are all works in progress.

Summing it Up:

- We need our church family and support systems (like the paralytic in the gospels).
- We grapple with our faith at times, but Jesus welcomes our mustard seed faith.
- The same God who created the universe has the glorious power to heal.
- Our spiritual and physical healing are part of a journey.
- There are many types of blindness in our lives. God opens our eyes.

Highlights from God's Word:

- Matthew 9:1-8; Mark 2:1-12; Luke 5:17-26
- Matthew 17:20
- Psalm 107:20-22
- Philippians 1:6
- Psalm 146:8; 2 Kings 6:17

Memos of Mountaintop Moments

Chapter 17
FROM MOURNING TO DANCING

You turned my wailing into dancing; you removed my sackcloth and clothed me with joy, that my heart may sing to you and not be silent. O Lord my God, I will give you thanks forever. Psalm 30:11-12

Keven had to take a moment and slip into a private room. For the first time in the nine years since his muscles had started to deteriorate, he was filled with emotion and grief. He had just performed the wedding of his foster daughter and was watching the father-daughter dance. One of his biological daughters was getting married the following year, and it dawned on him that not only would he not be able to participate in this special dance, he probably would not be able to walk her down the aisle.

After the sweet relief that pouring out your heart to God through tears can often bring, Keven rejoined the wedding festivities. Mourning his potential future did not change the convictions he had been living by. First, he would say with confidence to anyone who asked, "God is going to heal me." He didn't know when or how, but he knew he would either be restored on this earth or in his eternal home.

The other thing Keven often told others was, "My body is broken, but my faith is not." He knew God could use his story, and he was content to be where God had called him for this season. Keven didn't want anyone feeling sorry for him. God was continuing to be faithful. The rougher his pain and disability, the closer God drew him to His heart. The intimacy of God's presence became more important than his circumstances.

During the summer of 2009, Keven and his wife, Heidi, had attended an assembly of the General Church of the Nazarene in Florida. Within a day of returning home, Keven became violently ill. When his fever spiked dangerously two days later, he finally relented to being taken to urgent care. The medical staff met them in the parking lot with gloves and masks, ushered him into an isolated room, and confirmed what they suspected. Keven had contracted the Swine Flu. The doctor told him that he was lucky to be alive. Keven was sent home with medication, and took a total of two weeks off of work to recuperate.

Though Keven fully recovered from the flu, what he didn't know was that the severity of the disease had triggered an inflammation of his muscles. He later found out his muscular condition was called myositis. His muscles were slowly deteriorating, and since the heart is a muscle, most people with this condition die of heart failure. Unfortunately, Keven's doctors were unable to diagnose his condition for nine years. Keven and Heidi's journey into the unknown was just beginning.

In November of 2009, Keven turned forty years of age. He was bi-vocational, doing part-time youth ministry and part-time construction. He was used to playing a couple of basketball games a week with a group of twenty-somethings. He participated in softball leagues, hiking, golfing, and just about anything that was active and required athleticism. He had noticed that things were feeling a little off. Then, on the Sunday before Thanksgiving, he played flag football with the teens from church. The next day he could hardly move. He expected a little soreness, but this was extreme.

Keven made a doctor's appointment. The doctor chalked it up to his age, and gave him a prescription for some muscle relaxers. Keven didn't buy this explanation. For six months he kept insisting that something more was wrong. Finally, he was referred to a muscular specialist who ran several inconclusive tests. There just didn't seem to be any answers.

Over the next two years, Keven decided to concentrate on completing some ministerial studies. He had a needed shoulder surgery and lightened his activity level. Things just kept getting worse. Small movements were now bothering him. In 2012, they moved to Dinuba, where Keven became the senior pastor of a small church. The move meant that Heidi had given up her job with its benefits, so they started back on the journey of securing insurance and searching for local doctors.

The new doctor really listened, and another two-year cycle of testing ensued. The problem with suspected auto-immune diseases was that it often took years of tests to rule out one thing before they could move to the next. Three years later, there was still no definitive answer. Each CT scan, MRI, and x-ray would come back in the semi-normal range. However, by 2017, Keven was a shell of the person he had been. He was walking with a cane, sitting on a stool to preach, and could barely walk up a flight of stairs. The doctor told him he would just have to live like he was an eighty-five-year-old man.

Severe muscle cramps and spasms would wake Keven up during the night. He couldn't sleep more than forty-five minutes at a time without having to get up and walk around. He knew he wasn't sleeping deeply because he hadn't had a dream in years. REM sleep, or the dream state, follows non-REM sleep in which your boy builds bone and muscle, repairs and regenerates tissue, and strengthens the immune system. His body wasn't giving itself a chance to make these much needed adjustments throughout the night.

Even the lack of sleep, which Satan intended for evil, God used for good. Keven had been instructed by his doctor to get up and walk the house and stretch in the middle of the night. It was a horrible distraction and made resting even harder. During those times when the enemy wanted to remind Keven of his sickness, he began to pray for others. He prayed for his mom's cancer, his friend's battle with ALS, and anyone else that he knew was struggling with their health. The enemy's plan to discourage and defeat Keven became a time of solitude with God, a pattern that he still uses today whenever he is not able to sleep. Wakefulness becomes watchfulness. A restless body becomes a vigilant spirit.

In late 2017, Keven was referred to a neurologist. More tests were run, but this doctor was fairly certain that Keven had myositis. Keven googled the disease. He was shocked to read what his future body had in store. He began to run into individuals who knew of someone who had passed away from myositis. It almost always culminated in a heart attack or heart failure of some kind.

Keven and Heidi began to have some tough conversations. They had to look realistically at their future and what it would mean for Heidi and the kids if God didn't intervene. Heidi always believed in healing. It was difficult at times to watch Keven deal with his excruciating pain, but she never got to the place where she doubted God or felt totally distressed. Heidi had always believed in prayers for healing, and as a result they prayed together often.

They were both encouraged by others who prayed for them as well. It never failed that someone would send them a note or come up to them at an event to ask how Keven was doing, letting them know they were continuing to pray. Every time this happened, Keven would hear the very voice of God saying, "I have not forgotten you nor forsaken you. You are on My heart, and I have put you on theirs." God used the prayers of others as a soothing balm. These prayer warriors were vessels of God that helped keep Keven and Heidi going. As Keven put it, "They probably had no idea the impact they were making, but prayer makes a difference!"

The last test the doctor wanted to run to check his suspicions was a muscle biopsy. The procedure would require an incision in Keven's thigh. A circular piece of his quadricep muscle would be removed and sent to a UCLA lab for testing and confirmation. Keven experienced extreme pain post-biopsy, worse than anything he had suffered before. Every nerve in his body was sensitive to touch. It was as if his entire body was rebelling. It would be six weeks until the results would be back, so he waited and endured.

Two weeks after the procedure, Keven and Heidi were decorating their backyard for their foster-daughter's wedding. Keven prepared the spoken ceremony. The reception was to have a rustic theme, so they went to pick up some farm crates the Friday before the wedding. In a God-ordained moment, they met a perfect stranger. As conversation developed, Heidi found out that he had a miraculous story of being healed twice. She thought, "Who better to pray for the sick than someone who has been healed." Their new friend, Ed, was happy to pray over Keven.

Nothing significant happened at that moment. Keven and Heidi were eternally grateful for Ed's prayer. The wedding was beautiful, and the moment of brokenness that Keven had at the reception came and went. The following Tuesday, Keven woke up feeling "different." He couldn't pinpoint anything specific, but decided he was finally getting on the other side of the biopsy pain. As the week wore on, he kept monitoring his movements and energy level. On November 1, three weeks after his procedure, he went to his medicine drawer, filled with various prescriptions and pain relievers. He distinctly heard the voice of God speak to his inner being, "You don't need that medication. I have healed you."

Keven closed the drawer, told Heidi, and began to really pay attention to his body from a different perspective. By the time he went back for his muscle biopsy results, he knew he had been healed. He told Heidi before going in, "The doctor is going to tell me nothing's wrong."

After a few moments of small-talk, the doctor said they were going to talk about the results. "Mr. Huckaby, they have run every possible muscle test they can run. There is absolutely zero disease in your muscles."

Keven answered, "Well, doc, that's because God healed me." The doctor was skeptical. He shook his head a bit and said that this could be a time of remission, and please come back in six months. Keven was convinced that not only had God healed his body, but the Holy Spirit had gone into the UCLA lab, found his muscle sample, and healed it as well. There would be no remnant of this nine-year disease anywhere!

Keven began going to the gym with his son. He was lifting weights and building his strength and endurance back. A pivotal point came when he stood in front of a step to do a twelve-inch box jump. As he stood there, it was as if his feet could not move. He stepped back and asked God to help him. He squatted down, and hopped right on top of that box. He stood there for a while, on **higher ground**, with tears streaming down his face, not caring about the odd looks from the other gym members.

Keven distinctly remembers the morning he woke Heidi up yelling, "Heidi, I had a dream!" God had truly restored his body and mind. At his next six-month appointment, he hopped up on the doctor's table. He told the doctor how he was pumping iron, doing box jumps, and feeling great. The doctor stood there dumbfounded. He couldn't explain the transformation because God was the only explanation.

In October of 2019, he not only walked his daughter down the aisle, he danced with her. As if to put an exclamation point on the day, they put a few greased lightning moves into the middle of their waltz. God had turned his weeping from just a year ago into dancing. He was full of joy, and could not contain himself.

There is one more follow up to this story that is vitally important. In June of 2020, Keven woke up thinking he was having a heart attack. He lay there for a bit before waking Heidi to tell her of his symptoms. He showered and prepared for the day, but it wasn't getting better, so they went to an ER close by. All the tests showed that his heart was in perfect condition, so they reluctantly let him go home. Keven performed a funereal that day and preached the next, but he was still in a lot of pain across his chest. A nurse in his church told him to go to "her" ER, so the next morning they were back at it.

Everything he described pointed to a heart condition, so again, the tests were run. Results showed a perfect and strong heart. So, what was causing such excruciating pain and now the inability to catch a breath? It turns out, he had pleurisy, the symptoms of which mimic a heart attack. With the administration of steroids, they were able to reduce the pain and inflammation. Keven has had no further issues with this, but he now knows what to watch out for.

Keven and Heidi feel certain that God was once again showing them of his miraculous healing. The disease that was supposed to eat away at Keven's heart for almost a decade had left no trace. It was affirmed twice, by two different Emergency Rooms, that his heart muscle was perfect and whole. God does not do things halfway! Keven's heart could certainly withstand some more dancing.

Summing it Up:
- God has promised healing. We just don't know whether it will be on this earth or in our Heavenly home.
- In the midst of our pain, God draws us closer to His heart. The intimacy of God's presence becomes more important than our circumstances.
- In our toughest moments God says to us, "I have not forgotten you nor forsaken you. You are on My heart."

- God uses the prayers of others as a soothing balm and as vessels to keep us going. Prayer makes a difference!
- God turns our weeping into dancing, and we will give him thanks forever!

☀ Highlights from God's Word:

- Psalm 103:3; Revelation 21:4
- Psalm 145:18
- Deuteronomy 31:6
- James 5:16; Matthew 18:20
- Psalm 30:11-12

Memos of Mountaintop Moments

Chapter 18
ONE IN A MILLION

I praise you because I am fearfully and wonderfully made; your works are wonderful, I know that full well. Psalm 139:14

"You are one in a million!"

Most commonly, this phrase is a hyperbole used to refer to someone or something extraordinary or rare. The connotation is usually positive: "That diamond is one in a million," or "She is the sweetest person—she's one in a million."

When Debie heard these words, however, they were not what she was hoping to hear. Throughout 2005, Debie had been feeling increasingly weak. She was doing a lot of coughing, and the doctor had prescribed cough medicine and antibiotics for her symptoms, not once, but several times. As far as he was concerned, it should be working, but it obviously wasn't. She was forgetting things and became exhausted easily. One of her last symptoms was a sinus infection.

One morning, as she was getting out of bed, Debie could not stand up. Her legs buckled like a rag doll's. Her husband, Rob, saw her struggling and came to help. He gently guided her to a standing position, but her legs would not hold her up. A quick call to the doctor directed them to the hospital. It was the beginning of a six-week-long life-or-death journey.

Interestingly, Debie's general practitioner had a teacher long ago who would always talk about, "Churg-Strauss." He and his classmates thought it strange. Years later, Churg-Strauss came to her doctor's mind as he thought about her combined symptoms. This is a rare auto-immune disease which may affect multiple organ systems, especially the lungs. It is characterized by an abnormal clustering of certain white blood cells, eosinophils, and an inflammation of blood vessels. The symptoms mimic the flu, and Debie had many of these indicators, including fatigue, loss of appetite, weight loss, and muscle pain. After entering a local hospital, she lost over thirty pounds in two weeks as her red blood cells attacked and destroyed nerves and muscles throughout her body.

Debie's General Practitioner gathered the required specialists to check for the diagnosis. Only one in a million people have this disease, so the other doctors were skeptical. They wanted to check for other things first.

She was tested for Valley Fever, and they even told her daughter they were considering lung cancer. While waiting for the results from these tests, Debie's condition was worsening every day. They couldn't really treat her for one thing, in case it was another. The wrong treatment could literally kill her, but she was dying anyway. Her original doctor tried to have the necessary biopsies taken, but it was taking too long and she was fading fast.

Her doctor was trying to get Debie accepted by UCLA for a transfer to the university's hospital. It had been delayed three times. Rob finally took the bull by the horns. Gently, but firmly, not willing to take no for an answer this time, he asked to speak to the hospital manager. He explained what had been happening to his wife, looked the woman in the eyes, and said, "Look, if my wife doesn't get down to Los Angeles today, she is going to die."

God had ordained this meeting. The hospital manager in Bakersfield went above and beyond what had been done previously, and the transfer was arranged. Debie arrived at UCLA that night around 11:00 PM.

A few weeks later, Rob ran into the manager on the UCLA grounds. Surprised to see her, he asked what she was doing there. She explained that her son had been in a similar situation right around the time Rob had approached her. She knew exactly where his heart had been that day when he pleaded Debie's case. God's timing and scheduling put her in the right time and place that particular day.

On the day of Debie's transfer to UCLA, Rob watched as the EMTs placed his wife in the back of the ambulance. He wanted nothing more than to be alone with his thoughts on the way down to Los Angeles. He just needed to process all of this craziness with God. Instead, the ambulance staff insisted that he ride with them. Rob tried, several times, to refuse the offer, but they finally told him that they could not leave without him being in the front seat of the ambulance.

As Rob sat "shot-gun" in the ambulance, sure enough, the driver was ready to chat it up, the very thing that Rob was dreading. Rob was in inner turmoil. Then the driver asked him what he did for a living. When Rob explained that he was a pastor, it was as if, in the next few minutes, the driver was begging him to lead him to Christ. He began pouring out his heart, unsolicited, confessing the mess he had made of his life. Rob started to realize that God had a bigger picture in mind, relaxed into this new-established role for the moment, and shared the Gospel message of what Jesus had done for him.

Fearing they might run off the road due to the tears blurring the driver's vision, Rob was able to lead this hurting sin-sick individual into a relationship with the Lord. While Debie's body was in the back fighting for her physical life, Rob was in the front with a man who was fighting for his eternal life. God does not want anyone to perish, and He used this crisis in Rob and Debie's life to put him in a one-in-a-million position of leading an ambulance driver to life-giving first aid for His soul.

They arrived safely, and the university's state-of-the-art facility and staff kicked into high gear. All of the necessary biopsies were taken within 24 hours. Rob described the process and flow of activity as incredibly efficient. He referred to the staff as angels. Though it was probably just the jobs they did well from day to day, Rob was being infused with hope for the first time in quite a while. God was taking care of the big details of his wife's health, and he was taking care of the equally large details of Rob's emotions.

A staff member immediately took Rob into a waiting room as the medical staff took Debie into their care. The woman comforted Rob with assurance that things were going to be okay. She then looked at him and said, "I think you need some ice cream." She delivered a bowl of strawberry ice cream, Rob's favorite flavor, without him saying a word. Together they waited as the hospital ran their own tests on Debie, got results, and confirmed Churg-Strauss syndrome. Treatments began that very night. Debie was given high doses of prednisone and chemotherapy, which would taper off throughout the next eighteen months.

Debie was not out of the woods yet, but they finally had some answers and great hope for her recovery. She was in three hospitals for a total of forty-five days from the time she went that first day to the completion of her rehab, which included learning to walk again. From there, it took a couple more years of continually gaining strength and stamina. Debie declared she wouldn't change what she went through for anything. This is a theme that recurs with the stories in this book when people have been through trials. The closeness they feel to God as He draws them to **higher ground** during their trouble far surpasses the pain and suffering they have endured.

Rob and Debie would have missed witnessing the love and power of believers in prayer. People from their church would line up in the hall and be there just to pray. They received a call from someone in Louisiana who was praying for them, even though they did not know anyone in Louisiana. The prayer support and tangible acts of bringing food and goodies to fortify both body and soul for those who were waiting by Debie's bedside were constant and incredibly meaningful. God used others to remind them of His strength and help!

God brought someone to Debie's mind and heart, even though she was not fully conscious at the time. This someone lived far away, yet needed intercession. It was sounding like Debie was fervently praying for about fifteen minutes for this person who was so loved by God. Family members standing near her bed added to the fervent prayers, even though they weren't sure if Debie might be hallucinating or dreaming as they listened to her murmuring what seemed a bit nonsensical. They later found out that at the very moment Debie was praying, this dear one was contemplating suicide. She was saved from her demise through the prayer of a righteous one whose spirit was accustomed to being obedient to the promptings of the Spirit of God.

Days later, while he was waiting by Debie's bedside, God prompted Rob to call a man who had been a member of his previous church. Rob reasoned with God, "Now Lord? I don't even know this guy's phone number." Suddenly, a number popped into his brain, a number he couldn't tell you to this day. Upon dialing it, the man on the other end was exactly who God had told him to call. He was going through his own crisis, which at that very moment had reached a particular climax. Rob was able to share God's comfort with his friend through conversation and prayer, returning the comfort he had received through Christ and the body of believers.

Debie ended up giving up her career as a teacher because of the limitations of her body over the next months and years. As she gained strength, God opened another door that would not have crossed her mind if she had continued teaching. At an evangelism conference meeting, Debie felt the call on her heart and life to become a pastor. She didn't know how that would manifest itself since her husband was already a pastor. God continued to show her His way and brought her to her ordination day, eleven years after her journey with a rare disease.

Debie came to a place of sweet surrender. In so many ways, the illness paved the way for her to pursue a new calling and to be more cognizant of God's presence in her life than ever before. As a result of God's call, she is privileged to bring God's Word to churches across the Central California District. She is the director of ministerial studies and pastoral development for the district and oversees many of the district's special projects. God has used her as an instrument of His love and grace to bring many people to begin a new relationship with Christ and others to be renewed and strengthened in their relationship with Him.

Debie truly is one in a million. Like many of our Biblical examples, God allowed a trial in her life to draw her closer to God. Joseph went to jail, Daniel went to the lion's den, Paul was shipwrecked three times, and three Hebrew young men were thrown into a fiery furnace, just to list a few. Without these problems, they might not have come to a place of total dependency on God. We, too, can be that one in a million, who allows our trouble to draw us closer to God. He has designed us uniquely and wonderfully, creating us for a deep and abiding relationship with Him.

Summing it Up:

- God does not want anyone to perish, and He can use our own crises to place us in just the right time and place to lead someone into a life-giving relationship with the Lord.
- As He draws us to Himself during our trouble, the closeness of God far surpasses the pain and suffering we endure.
- We need each other's prayer support and tangible acts to fortify our bodies and souls during times of crises. God uses others to remind us of His strength and help!
- We need to be in tune with the Spirit of God, listening to His promptings to pray for others.
- We are given opportunities, if we will listen to God's voice, to be a comfort to others because of the comfort Christ has given to us.

- God has designed us uniquely and wonderfully, creating us for a deep and abiding relationship with Him.

☀ Highlights from God's Word:
- 2 Peter 3:9
- Psalm 23:4; Psalm 34:18
- Philippians 1:3-4; 4:14
- James 5:16
- 2 Corinthians 1:4
- Psalm 139:14

Memos of Mountaintop Moments

Chapter 19

When I am Weak

That is why, for Christ's sake, I delight in weaknesses, in insults, in hardships, in persecutions, in difficulties. For when I am weak, then I am strong. 2 Corinthians 12:10

Scott had never felt weaker than when he was receiving his cancer treatments. He had also never been more buoyed by the presence of the Holy Spirit. He recognized his need for complete surrender to God. He immersed himself in scriptures, listening to cassette tapes over and over again, absorbing God's promises. He played worship music that filled his soul. Life had been stripped down to a hospital room and Christ, and Scott felt the overwhelming presence of God with him.

It started in the winter of 1996. Scott went to see his doctor in Baker City, Oregon, for a sinus infection. After a couple rounds of antibiotics, he was not getting better. In fact, besides the stuffy nose, he started experiencing frequent nose bleeds, something he never remembered having in over thirty years of life. After six months of no relief, Scott was sent to an ear, nose, and throat (ENT) specialist in the next town over.

The doctor in La Grande, Oregon, took one look and knew it was a situation to be concerned about. He took a tissue sample which came back positive for squamous cell carcinoma, stage four cancer. Admitting that this was way beyond his expertise, the ENT referred

Scott to Oregon Health Science University (OHSU) for further diagnosis and treatment.

In July of 1996, Scott and his wife, Denise, along with their two little boys, ages three and seven, packed up for the journey to Portland. They planned to stay with Denise's parents while Scott was examined. They left in a hurry, with their doors unlocked, food in the fridge, and their dog in the backyard. This was urgent, and they felt they shouldn't wait. The only thing they did wait on was for their friends from church to come over and pray for them. The prayers of these saints and others around the world would be their lifeblood over the next few months.

At OHSU, the university's teaching hospital in Portland, the tissue sample was again analyzed, along with a series of other assessments. Scott was set up with an otolaryngologist, a physician trained in the medical and surgical care of head and neck disorders, including cancers. His oncology regimen was to include three months of chemo treatments.

Scott became very sick and weak with each ensuing chemo treatment. Denise was left to pay the bills, deal with the boys, update Scott's workplace of his progress, and handle any major decisions. These tasks would have buried her had it not been for the continued prayers and support of her family and friends. This was an age prior to easy access to cell phones and emails. All correspondence had to be done through the mail or by long distance phone calls. Over the course of the next few months, they received hundreds upon hundreds of encouraging notes from their church body, six hours away.

Denise's mom helped her tape the cards to ribbon and string them from the ceiling all around Scott's room. He was literally surrounded by scripture and prayer as he lay there. They purchased a United States map and began putting pins in the places where people were praying for them. One friend would share their need with a friend or relative in another part of the country. Before the ordeal was over, there were very few spots on the map without a pin. The prayers of many made such a difference!

They began to see the hand of God in the middle of their trial. Scott's company, a workers' compensation organization for which he was a consultant, allowed him to use all of his earned time, vacation days and sick leave. When that was used up, they set up a program in which his co-workers could donate their own sick leave and vacation days. Scott was gone a total of six months. He attests to God's goodness as he reflected that he did not miss a pay check the entire time.

Unfortunately, the MRI that was conducted in October at the end of his first set of chemo treatments showed that it had done nothing to shrink the tumor. The next step was to start radiation. This was intended to just keep things at bay for as long as possible. The doctors wanted to keep Scott comfortable, focusing on quality of life over quantity of years. This was not the news they had hoped for. They were young parents of two little boys. Scott was not afraid to die, but he was afraid to leave his family alone.

Denise assured him they would be okay. Scott's senior pastor had a heart-to-heart phone conversation with him, telling him it was time to let go, to surrender 100% to God. He had nothing to lose at this point. Scott felt like his faith had been strong, now it was time to instill a strong trust.

In the meantime, God was working through Denise's brother. He was an oral surgeon and had contact with colleagues across the country. Through these contacts, he had found out about an experimental treatment in Memphis, which focused on Scott's exact type of cancer. Through investigating further and getting paperwork started, they found out they had been accepted into this research program's trial study. Word came as they were pulling out of the driveway for his first radiation treatment. Denise's mom came running out to tell them there was a phone call. God's timing was perfect as they were stopped before the car left the house. If Scott had gone through even one radiation treatment that day, his case would have been disqualified.

Getting insurance approval was next. Their HMO needed to review the case in order to prequalify payments. To get started in a timely manner, Scott and Denise needed to come up with $30,000 up front. Word spread across the network of friends and family, without Facebook or Paypal or Venmo. Enough money was wired to the hospital's account in time for the procedure to begin.

The doctors in Memphis scheduled what was called RadPlat Therapy. It was a combination of daily radiation and four doses of the chemo drug called Cisplatin. This was a chemo drug that was injected right into the tumor itself. The strength of this dose would most likely kill the patient if given systemically (through the entire body). It was counteracted by an antidote given by IV that neutralized the cisplatin to the rest of the body. This allowed the chemo that was injected right into the tumor to do the job without hurting the rest of the body. As Scott was getting wheeled in for the first "dose" of this state-of-the-art therapy, they got word that their insurance had approved the treatments. They had no out-of-pocket expenses from that day forward.

Before heading to Memphis, a dear friend, described as one who was very in tune with the Holy Spirit, spoke a special word into their lives. She encouraged them to look everywhere for God. In essence, she was saying, "Open the eyes of your heart to see how God is working and caring for you in the midst of your trial." The results of being cognizant of God's hand going before them and being with them were amazing.

Denise was very nervous about having to drive through a new city and find her way around. Two of the streets near the Memphis hospital had names with strong associations to her life back home. It was a small signpost, but it gave her such comfort. One of the residents who was working on Scott was Dr. Neno. Neno was the "grandma" name given to their friend who had given them the advice about looking for God. They visited a local Memphis church. This congregation of about 1000 "strangers" gathered around them for prayer, anointed Scott, and spent the next few weeks visiting, calling, and caring for this couple who were in a new city with no former contacts. They were seeing God!

God also revealed how He had been working all along. The new school teacher for their second-grade son listened as Denise shared what they were going through, and that their son, Zach, would be there on a temporary basis for the beginning of the school year. The teacher reached into a drawer and pulled out a picture of Jesus holding a lamb. She assured this family that she would be praying for them, and that Jesus was holding them and their kids.

Although the insurance company took care of the expenses, Denise had to make multiple calls as the hospital bills started streaming in. It was difficult to make sense of it all. In her initial contact with the insurance company, she was connected with a wonderful Christian woman who not only prayed for them, but she insisted that Denise only work through her. She was familiar with the case and helped Denise keep on top of all the craziness of the billings.

Bills that needed to be paid at home were being routed through their home address to Portland, and now to Memphis. The utility companies were willing to work with them, knowing that some of the payments would be coming in late due to the circumstances. Utilities were never turned off. The church community took care of their dog, mowed their lawn, shoveled snow, and kept things running smoothly on the home front the entire time they were gone.

More cards of encouragement streamed into the apartment they were staying at in Memphis. Scott continued to be sick and weak throughout the four treatments of chemo and the daily radiation. Even through that time, God showed up through an eighty-five-year-old man who shared the same radiation appointment time with Scott. As they were waiting for their turn, this man would praise God and speak truth and love into Scott's life, encouraging Him in the Lord.

At the end of the experimental treatment protocol, they waited for the results of his MRI. In order to do the final step of surgery, the cancer mass had to have shrunk enough to be able to remove it without placing the optic nerves in danger. The anticipated results came in. It had shrunk significantly. They were able to schedule the surgery for the first of the year. By now it was the tenth of December. Their plan was to go home and surprise the boys for Christmas.

After a joyful reunion and beautiful Christmas in Portland, Denise and Scott headed back to Memphis. Denise's brothers came to sit with her through the ten-hour surgery. There was a risk of stroke during the surgery, so they were there to offer their support. Before going under, the doctor explained that he would be making an incision in Scott's upper forehead in the shape of an angel's wings. The heavenly scar on Scott's forehead remains as another sign that God was keeping him covered.

After opening his forehead, the neurosurgeon cut a section of his skull out to expose and push back the frontal lobe of his brain. From there the oncologist could go in through the top and remove the tumor. They sent tissue samples all along the way to test them for live cancer cells. They gave the family in the waiting room hourly updates of how things were going. When the surgery concluded, there was not one live cancer cell in any of the tissue samples.

The morning after surgery, Denise was waiting to be told she could go see Scott in his ICU room. The doctors had tried to prepare her for the fact that he would have a huge bandage around his head. He might be on a ventilator. He would probably be out of it. While she was waiting, she received a call...from Scott...wondering where she was. He was most upset at the fact that there was no television in the room. It was Sunday, and there was a football game he wanted to watch.

After a sufficient recuperation, Scott was medically released. They went back to Portland, gathered their boys, and with a caravan of cars and vans from the church, they made the six-hour trek home. Six months after this ordeal had begun, Scott was healed and ready to get back to work. As they arrived at the one exit of their little town, a few rogue cars came up from behind, eased into the lead, and slowed the caravan down. The little family thought it was a bit odd, but kept on going.

As they made their way onto the main street of town, hundreds of people were lining both sides of the street. Church members, community members, sports teams, and friends of their kids cheered and welcomed them home. Even though many shared with them later what an inspiration their journey had been to them, Scott and Denise felt like they were the recipients of the blessing and inspiration. They were overwhelmed and lifted to **higher ground** through the love, support, and prayers of God's people.

Summing it Up:

- When we recognize our need for complete surrender to God, we will be immersed in God's overwhelming presence.
- The prayers of many make such a difference!
- We must open the eyes of our heart to see how God is working and caring for us in the midst of our trials.

Highlights from God's Word:

- Phil. 4:13; 2 Corinthians 12:10
- Matthew 18:20
- Ephesians 1:18-19

Memos of Mountaintop Moments

Chapter 20
IT'S YOURS

Therefore I tell you, whatever you ask for in prayer, believe that you have received it, and it will be yours. Mark 11:24

Picture a child who has submitted his or her request for a prized Christmas or birthday gift. They wait expectantly, and a little impatiently, in the weeks and days leading up to the big day. They repeatedly remind their mom and dad of their desired wish. There may be moments when they doubt it is coming, but then the anticipated day comes. The parents have thoughtfully purchased and wrapped the gift. They are just as excited as the child who is about to open the present.

Then, something unexpected happens. The child tears into the wrapping. She looks at the item, exactly what she had asked for, but she claims that she just can't believe it is hers. Not only can she not believe it, but she refuses to accept it. She feels it is undeserved. She is worried that it might break if she picks it up.

Of course, this is a ridiculous scenario. There would actually be smiles and hugs and kisses all around. Yet that is how we sometimes pray. We ask God for healing or strength or peace or wisdom, but we don't really believe it will happen. We miss out on the smiles and love because somehow our doubts and sense of unworthiness take over.

Heidi (wife to Keven in "From Mourning to Dancing," Chapter 17) was nineteen years old when she learned this lesson about praying, believing, and accepting an answer in faith. Her story takes the cake (or hamburger, in this case). She had worked her way up after high school to become the manager of a local Wendy's restaurant. She was making quite a bit of money in her managerial position. Life was looking good!

Heidi had not been raised attending church. Her mom was part of a church that she attended periodically whose beliefs were grounded in some branch of scientology. It was a kind of feel good, "Kumbaya"-type of religion. Nevertheless, morals were taught in the home, and Heidi remembers her mom singing "How Great Thou Art" and "I Come to the Garden Alone" at bedtime.

A high school friend tried to witness to her, but her idea of salvation came more in the flavor of hell and damnation rather than freedom and salvation. Regardless, Heidi was open to things of God. She was surprised to look back on her essays from a high school psychology class where she wrote about God a lot. She was seeking, and God's fingerprints were on her life all along the way.

One night, while she was closing the books at the Wendy's restaurant, a couple of hired gentlemen came in to paint some back rooms of the store. One of the guys was young, and kind of cute, so Heidi went out of her way to be friendly. They had some good conversation before she went back to her tallying tasks. The next evening, she was looking forward to seeing them again. It appeared at first like they were not going to be back, but she suddenly got the whiff of fresh paint. She knew they had returned.

Once again, she greeted them, wanting them to feel appreciated and welcome. Their conversation continued from the night before, one question leading to the next. The men shared the gospel with her and led her to Christ that night. Painters for Jesus portrayed the many hues of a Christ who loved and died for her. It doesn't matter what we do for a living, Jesus can use our lives to share the Good News with others. Heidi asked forgiveness, accepted Jesus as her Lord, and received the free gift of eternal life that night.

The next day, Heidi spoke to her boss. She asked for Sundays off. She was a Christian now and she needed to go to church. He firmly told her that managers don't get the weekends off. She kindly let him know she was going to have to quit. He didn't want to lose this valuable employee. When he found out she needed Sunday nights for the evening service and Wednesday nights for Bible study, you can imagine his dilemma. Surprised by her resolve, the boss amazingly worked it out so that she could work a noon to five o'clock shift on Sundays and have Wednesday nights off as well.

Heidi would attend church in her striped Wendy's uniform each Sunday morning. She would sit near the back so that she could dart out and get to work. She was learning and growing in Christ, and she recognized in her spiritual infancy the importance of being part of a body of believers. Too often we are swayed by the fact that we have been hurt or shamed by a church. A Facebook "blog" that was recently posted by an up-and-coming speaker and friend, Lauren Vasser, recognized that many people resolve to never set foot in a church again.

She goes on to describe the church as a place full of people, and people are flawed. This means, "no matter if you are at church or a club...you will encounter imperfect people who do dumb things. Period. Don't let that keep you from the gift of church. The church isn't perfect. It's a community. A flawed group of imperfect people who need Jesus. Don't look for a perfect church, or even a church with the best preacher. It doesn't exist. Look for a church who desperately seeks God."

Heidi recognized the church as a gift. She found other Jesus-seekers and surrounded herself with them. She was bold in her faith then, and she is strong in her convictions today, decades later, as a pastor's wife. In the story of her husband's healing, she was as encouraged as he was by the church, the people of God, who prayed for them and listened to God's promptings.

Still new to her Christian journey, Heidi learned about the power of prayer and healing. As a young adult, she was having "female problems." When she went to have things checked, a lump was discovered on her right ovary. The doctor ordered tests. Blood work was done, and x-rays were taken. One of the things Heidi immediately did was knock on the door of the nearest church. When it was answered, she explained her problem and asked for prayer.

Later, while Heidi waited back at the hospital waiting room for the results of the tests, she took out her Bible. She is not even sure where she got it, but when she opened the black hard-back Bible she had acquired from somewhere, a note was in the front. It was in her handwriting, but she had no recollection of writing it. It simply had a verse inscribed, Mark 11:24.

Curious, she opened to the verse. It said, "Therefore I tell you, whatever you ask for in prayer, believe that you have received it, and it will be yours" (Mark 11:24). Heidi reflected on the meaning of the verse for her present circumstance. She realized that she had prayed for healing, but she hadn't believed that she had received it. It was like the child opening the Christmas gift but not accepting it as hers.

She said a silent prayer as she sat in the waiting room chair. She confessed that she had not really believed that the healing would happen. She prayed anew that the lump would be healed, and she declared that she believed God had already done it. Her prayer was interrupted by a nurse calling her name to come on back.

The intern who had originally seen her let her know that because he was still in his residency, he couldn't schedule surgery without getting two other doctors' opinions. However, he still wanted to do the first exam to compare the results of the tests. As he felt for the lump, he looked puzzled. He asked Heidi if maybe it was on her left side, even though the x-rays he was glancing up at showed where it was. There was nothing on either side. Heidi smiled and told him her story of healing. There was medical proof, pictures of the lump, and now it was gone!

Heidi continued to grow in the Lord. She eventually met and married Keven. His salvation story is as riveting, though different from Heidi's. He was walking a path of wild living. He had grown up in a dysfunctional home where his mom basically raised him alone. His dad was absent most of the time, and had a problem with alcoholism. His mom had strayed from the church, but was starting to attend and straighten her life out. She had asked Keven to go with her one Sunday morning.

He woke up that Sunday, after a night of partying, feeling way too hungover to go. He went into the bathroom to wash his face, and then he was going to call his mom with the disappointing news that he wasn't feeling well this morning. As he looked into the mirror, he saw his father looking back at him. He had vowed he would not become like his dad, and yet here he was, behaving the same way. Keven forced himself to get ready and met his mom for church. He heard the gospel message that morning, and he was transformed, body, soul, and spirit.

Once Keven and Heidi started a family, Keven was determined that he would be a great dad to his two little girls. One of their girls, Sierra, was about two years old. She developed a terrible cough. The doctor said it was asthma, and that she would suffer with it all her life. She would wake up in the night, hacking and wheezing at the side of her crib.

One night, as they were getting ready for bed, Keven turned on "The 700 Club." "The 700 Club," which first broadcast in 1966, is a newsmagazine featuring guests, news, music, testimonies and spiritual stories from a Christian perspective. This particular night the host, Pat Robinson, was ending a segment. He said, "Right now someone has a little girl with asthma. God is healing her right now." Keven felt a quickening in his spirit.

He turned to Heidi and said, "He is talking about our Sierra." They held hands and prayed, believing that God had sent this word to them. Even though the program had been pre-recorded, God used that specific moment to build their faith and prove his faithfulness. Sierra, as the parents described, never coughed again. Of course, she had a common cold here and there, but there was never any more asthma.

Jesus healed many people during His three years of ministry on Earth. Crowds were drawn to Him because of His miraculous powers and signs. In one such episode, some men brought a paralytic to Jesus. When He saw their faith, He said to the paralytic, "Take heart, son, your sins are forgiven" (Matthew 9:2b).

There were some teachers of the law standing nearby who accused Jesus of blaspheming or disrespecting God. Jesus knew their thoughts and He said, "Which is easier to say, 'Your sins are forgiven,' or to say, 'Get up and walk'?" (Matthew 9:5).

Then to show His authority, Jesus admonished the man to take up his mat and go home, which he did. The crowd was filled with awe and praised God. We, like the crowd, are in awe when we see miracles take place. God is still in the miracle business today.

He is also in the business of transforming hearts and lives. Are we as much in awe when someone gives their heart to Christ as we are when we see a "physical" sign of healing? The Bible doesn't say what happens in Heaven when there is a healing of someone's body. It is clear, however, that when a sinner repents, there is a Heavenly party with the angels in the presence of God.

It is important to ask in prayer for God to heal. It is equally, and even more important to ask for God to heal a person's soul and restore them as a new creature in Christ. Both prayers require steadfastness and belief. God answers and lifts our faith and trust to **higher ground**. Pray and believe. Open God's gifts and believe that they will be yours!

Summing it Up:
- It doesn't matter what we do for a living, Jesus can use our lives to share the Good News with others.
- The church isn't perfect. It's a community. A flawed group of imperfect people who need Jesus. Don't look for a perfect

church, or even a church with the best preacher. It doesn't exist. Look for a church who desperately seeks God."
- The Bible is clear that when a sinner repents, there is a Heavenly party with the angels in the presence of God.
- Our prayers require steadfastness and belief. God answers and lifts our faith and trust to **higher ground**. Pray and believe. Open God's gifts and believe that they will be yours!

☀ Highlights from God's Word:

- Mark 16:15
- Hebrews 10:25
- Luke 15:10
- Mark 11:24

Memos of Mountaintop Moments

Choosing Higher Ground

Chapter 21
HINDSIGHT IS 2020

...But one thing I do: Forgetting what is behind and straining forward for what is ahead, I press on toward the goal...
Philippians 3:13-14a

I'm so glad God didn't choose 2020 to have me fast coffee! In my first book, *Common Ground,* I share how God's prompting to fast coffee led to me becoming an author. God and I fought for a couple of days about the necessity of giving up the black liquid refreshment, but ultimately, I recognized it was really Him speaking. For twenty-one days, I put God before my desire to drink coffee each morning, and He planted within me the idea of writing the Coffee Shop Chronicles. I think it would have put me under if fasting coffee had been God's directive for me during the pandemic.

I remember exactly where I was when the news came that California had been hit by the coronavirus. It was the last week of February, and we were finishing up a week-long writing retreat. A couple of the participants were catching a flight out of the Sacramento airport. We received word that the first cases of Covid-19 had been reported in Sacramento County.

Our hostess ensured that everyone left with an arsenal of personal snacks and disinfectant wipes. In the ensuing weeks, things started to snowball:

- Trips, retreats, and special events like graduations and weddings were canceled

- Schools closed
- Zoom meetings became the norm
- TP, Paper towels, and hand sanitizers became elusive
- People we knew were being hospitalized...a few didn't make it
- Masks became part of our apparel
- Our country was experiencing extreme social unrest

I kept rehearsing the words, "Everything's going to be OK." But my heart hadn't caught up with my head yet. I was feeling depressed and discouraged, mixed with a fair amount of despair. I felt physically isolated, mentally quarantined, and emotionally angry.

There was no apparent end in sight. I know I wasn't alone, and guilt added to my despair because so many of my issues seemed selfish. Lots of people had it worse than me! But the reality was still mine, and God was working on my faith through the fire. It was a slow and steady process.

Through this time, staying grounded in God's Word was vitally important! I can't emphasize enough the importance of the discipline of daily Bible study! Just about the time I didn't think I could keep going, I would read a passage of scripture that would spur me on, reminding me of who Jesus is and who I am in Him.

Looking back through my journal, I can now see how God was molding and teaching me through the entire year. Here are some of the paraphrased entries.

April—For the first time in my life we weren't able to go to church (in person) on Easter Sunday. We were also ramping up prayers for Al Vaughn (see Chapter 11), who was in ICU dealing with Covid. Defeat seemed to be surrounding us.

I needed to experience victory through Christ. I went to God's Word and focused and repeated these verses:

"But God raised him from the dead, freeing him from the agony of death, because it was impossible for death to keep its hold on him" (Acts 2:24).

"And if the Spirit of him who raised Jesus from the dead is living in you, he who raised Christ from the dead will also give life to your mortal bodies through his Spirit who lives in you" (Romans 8:11).

The same power that raised Christ from the dead was available to me. What Satan thought was the defeat of his foe was the path to Christ's victory. I could participate in that victory through Christ!

May—I had cabin fever. Weary of being cooped up at home, we decided to drive out to the Antelope Valley Poppy Reserve one Sunday afternoon. The visitor center was closed, but people parked their cars on the side of the road and walked up the hills to get a closer look at the spectacular display of God's glory!

After the wonderful early April rains, the hills were alive with wildflowers. The sight of the bright orange poppies and purple lupines was exhilarating. It felt fresh and new and vibrant. This verse came to mind: "Therefore, if anyone is in Christ, he is a new creation; the old has gone, the new has come!" (2 Corinthians 5:17).

I had new inspiration to stop looking inward, focusing on the old, and start celebrating the new.

June—I was definitely starting to grumble! When was this thing (Covid-19 and its restrictions) going to lift!?! Summer was upon us and we NEEDED a chance to vacation and play.

As I stewed over all the unfortunate events, God brought this passage to mind: "But the fruit of the Spirit is love, joy, peace, patience, kindness, goodness, faithfulness, gentleness, and self-control. Against such things there is no law" (Galatians 5:22-23). The fruit of the Spirit was familiar to me, since I have done life with Jesus for a while.

When I pray for these traits to become a part of my life, I am, more often than not, given a chance to practice them. If I pray for patience, the Lord shows me an opportunity to display love and grace in a situation that would otherwise find me totally irritated. When I pray for joy to overflow through me, He reminds me, when I am getting ready to grumble, that I can choose to delight in people and circumstances because God is with me. I focused on finding victory through Christ's character and began to pray for peace and gentleness in my life. God was working on me, and slowly chiseling away at areas I needed to change.

July—July was promising to bring no relief. There were to be no 4th of July gatherings, no Family Camp, just more of the same restrictions and exasperating news. We were half way through 2020...and what a year it had been thus far!

The apostle Paul knew a little about days like this, days of uncertainty and hardship. He wrote in Philippians that he had learned to be content, whatever the circumstances. He knew what it meant to be in need. He also knew what it meant to have plenty.

But he had learned a great secret. No matter what he was going through, he could get through it because of Christ! (See Philippians 4:13)

God was reminding me, once again through the promises in the Bible, that whatever the second half of 2020 was to bring, I could trust God to give me the strength to get through the days ahead.

August —We found out we were going to have our local grandkids full time for the school year. I began going through a time of grief and mourning. I greatly missed my early mornings alone. My time to walk, exercise, and leisurely sit outside on my patio with God's Word was coming to a screeching halt. I was grieving for our nation. I was grieving over lives lost to Covid and its effects. I was disheartened because of the loss of socialization and in-person school days my grandchildren would be experiencing.

I was grieving, as I did each year during California's wildfire season, over homes being destroyed, stately forests being burned to the ground, and lives being snuffed out before their time. The smoke from the fires made its home at the base of the southern Sierras where we live. Our air quality was awful! I grieved over not being able to take a deep breath of air when I stepped outside.

In the midst of this grieving, I viewed a picture someone had taken of the sunrise, shrouded in the smoky haze. The scene was eerily beautiful. It reminded me that even in the midst of the trial, God promises us beauty for ashes (Isaiah 61:3). I claimed God's oil of gladness. The blessed assurance of this promise brought such hope.

October—One of the huge benefits of having our grandkids each day was that we had about an hour each morning to fill before school started. Once we realized that they were going to need a little structure when they arrived, we began having family devotions. Our six-year-old grandson would walk through the house declaring, "It's time for family emotions!"

As we came to the end of the Sermon on the Mount found in Matthew's gospel, the kids seemed familiar with the last bit about the wise and foolish builders. This time, however, we discussed it in the context of all the other things we had read in the previous weeks.

We played "My Feet are on the Rock," by I Am They, and rocked out a bit. (What a far cry from the song I sang in Sunday School about how the rains came tumbling down.) We talked about what our foundation in Christ meant. He will never let you down. The storms of life cannot topple your house. We were able to apply it to what was going on in our world right then. It was a great reminder and a wonderful truth for us to be able to share with our grandkids.

November—We were getting close to Thanksgiving and we still didn't seem to see an end to school closures. They tried implementing a soft opening for a few weeks, but cases of Covid spiked, so they closed them back up. As we prayed each morning, it was amazing how our grandkids showed their simple trust in a powerful God.

Psalm 8:2 proclaims, "From the lips of children and infants you have ordained praise because of your enemies, to silence the foe and the avenger." I'm not sure I really understood the second half of that verse until I heard our six-year-old grandson pray one morning: "I pway [he's working on his r's] for all the wicked people, that they would turn good and know about the Bible." WOW! We should be praying for our enemies and silencing the foe with the love and righteousness granted by Jesus, who came as a child and led us into God's kingdom of peace and love. It took a child to remind me of this amazing privilege.

December—Christmas was coming. I didn't even put up a tree, since we weren't having a family gathering. It was easy to contemplate what that first Christmas must have been like. Mary had to have been in turmoil, but excited about the Son of God in her womb.

When Mary visited her relative, Elizabeth, she received affirmation and blessing (see Luke 1:45). Mary then sang a song. In the King James version, Mary says, "My soul doth magnify the Lord" (Luke 1:46).

When something is magnified, it is seen as greater than everything else around it. It reminded me that during the Christmas season, and all year long, we should lift the Lord in praise. We should magnify Him! By remembering to put Him first and see Him as greater than all our circumstances, our problems are put into proper perspective.

So, as I look in hindsight at the year 2020, I learned how to rise above the muck of life onto **higher ground**. I learned to live in victory in spite of the circumstances that were attempting to beat me down. God slowly, but surely, was gracious to remind me that through Him and His Word, I could experience victory. Victory arose through focusing on Christ's character, His strength, His comfort, His presence, His power, and His wisdom. Perhaps the greatest lesson I learned was to experience victory through praise, forgetting what lies behind and magnifying the Lord.

Summing it Up:

- The same power that raised Christ from the dead is available to us.
- We need to stop looking inward, focusing on the old, and celebrate the new.
- When we focus finding victory through Christ's character and begin to pray for the fruit of the Spirit to reign in our lives, God will faithfully work on us, and slowly chisel away at the areas we need to change.
- No matter what we are going through, we can get through it because of Christ!
- Even in the midst of the trial, God promises us beauty for ashes.
- Our foundation in Christ will get us through the storms of life.
- We should be praying for our enemies and silencing the foe with the love and righteousness granted by Jesus.
- We should daily magnify the Lord! By remembering to put Him first and see Him as greater than all our circumstances, our problems are put into proper perspective.

Highlights from God's Word:

- Acts 2:24; Romans 8:11
- 2 Corinthians 5:17
- Galatians 5:22-23
- Philippians 4:13
- Isaiah 61:3
- Matthew 7:24-27

- Psalm 8:2
- Luke 1:46; Philippians 3:13-14

Memos of Mountaintop Moments

Chapter 22

RISE

Early the next morning they arose and worshiped the Lord.
I Samuel 1:19a

The first time I adopted a "word for the year" was in 2021. It wasn't something I had taken a part in before. I'm not sure why or how my 2021 word came to me, but I felt like the word "Bless" was placed on my heart. I knew I wanted 2021 to be a year of blessing, but I sensed that the word needed to be an action word. It wasn't about me receiving blessings, but finding ways to give a blessing to others: bless the Lord; bless those on Facebook; bless my family; bless those I met along the way throughout my day. Blessing meant looking out for the interest of others.

I reached out to my Facebook group and asked them to share their word of the year. I was pleasantly surprised at the responses. One friend chose "purposeful." She hoped to be purposeful in seeking the Lord, in serving, and in her habits. Another friend, recently retired, decided to hang on to the word "diligent." She desired that her new routines would be enveloped in diligence for the Lord and in her daily activities. A third chose "courage." She wanted to face the unknown and unexpected circumstances with courage. She wanted to be able to do the right thing, and to overcome fears that stopped her from doing just that. She wanted to be able to love the unlovable and to go forward from losses with bravery. A final word worth mentioning was "thankful." This friend had some scary health issues the previous year, and those situations framed her thoughts of being thankful to be alive, to have all she needs, to be able to share with others, to have a wonderful husband and family by her side, and to have friends!

We tend to choose a word based on our current or most recent circumstances. Sometimes, however, we receive a God-given word that He will use to reveal more of Himself to us throughout the coming days, weeks, and months. I ran across Lindsay's word in May of 2021. Like me, it was the first time she had tried this practice. With her permission I am sharing her Facebook post:

> "I've never been a 'word for the year' person. I love the idea of it, but I never took the time to pray or process one of my own. When the new year started, I kept hearing the word RISE, so I adopted it.
>
> "I lost sight of that word come March. On February 25th I found out I was pregnant. Never in my life did I think I would get a positive test. I had just been explaining to a friend how frustrating pregnancy symptoms are because they're the same as PMS. The next day I took a test and it was positive. I waited a day, took another, again positive. I told Jer [her husband] on Wednesday night. I cried. After trying for a year and 8 months, we were finally pregnant. I was anxious and excited all week. I had a doctor's appointment scheduled for the following week with a new fertility specialist so we decide we'd wait until then to tell immediate family and a couple friends. That whole week we had been calling our baby a girl. I just felt like she was and so did Jer.
>
> "On March 1st, I woke up and realized I miscarried. And I physically felt it all day. It was incredibly painful. We took

off to the beach despite the pain I was experiencing, to spend time together and grieve. All our hopes and dreams flew out the window. I had prayed over her all week, begging her to stay, to get cozy in there so we could meet her come November 4th. We tried to not get excited, but you can't help it. It's easier said than done. Driving home it dawned on me that 31 years ago to the day, my mom lost Baby K, my older brother. He was born with Anencephaly. How crazy that we would both lose a baby on the same day.

"There's a lot more to my story that I'd like to share. So much has happened since March 1st. Somewhere in the midst of my grief I remembered my word for this year, and I've pushed forward. For me, for us, for her, for our future babies. But for today, I wanted to share with the world that we had a daughter, who we loved more than we knew was humanly possible. For the week we knew about her, she was loved and prayed for and wanted. I never knew you could love and miss something so tiny. I wish I could have met her and held her. She made me a mom and I can't wait to meet her one day."

A couple of days after Lindsay's miscarriage, she went to her previously arranged appointment with the new infertility specialist. She sensed God's perfect timing as she met with this doctor, explaining her past year and a half of unsuccessful attempts at pregnancy, ending in her recent loss. The doctor did a thorough investigation, delved into her medical history, and ran a series of tests that no other doctor had done previously. When tested for four particular antibodies that could inhibit pregnancy, Lindsay tested positive for two of them.

What this meant was that her body treated the embryo like an invasive tissue. Blood clots would form and her body would go about its business to kill the embryo. Lindsay began a regimen of medications and treatments which included giving herself injections three days after ovulation. New treatments and a doctor who seemed to really listen and care brough such hope.

Eventually, however, it felt like insult was being added to injury when each month's testing would not reveal a pregnancy. Instead, the visible results were only bruises all over her stomach from her shots. Lindsay admitted to living a roller coaster of emotions. One minute she would be angry with God. (Before casting judgment, a quick look at the Psalms reveals David often spoke out in anger to God about his circumstances.) Then, like David, Lindsay would move forward in trust, knowing God would fulfill the desires of her heart. She would be reminded of her word "rise." Sometimes ascending to this place of **higher ground** meant just getting out of bed. Other times it meant moving forward in the day, even when it was hard. Praise songs often included the word "rise," and was a reminder that she could rely on the God of promises, one day at a time.

Lindsay often showed her gratefulness to God for making her the resilient person she was becoming. Life never seemed easy. She had some tough situations growing up. Her husband, Jer, was having physical issues that put him in and out of the hospital. Her dream teaching job, getting to share her passion of music with students, was abruptly ended due to the Covid shut-downs. Her band was unable to perform the spring concert that they had worked so hard to prepare for all year.

Her resilience helped her push through once again. She was able to see the time off from work as an opportunity to complete her credential classes. She used the time to study for her three multiple subject California Subject Examinations for Teachers (CSET's) that she needed to pass. It also gave her the chance to finish up a series of master's classes in English Language Learning. At the present time, the only hurdle left is passing two music CSET's. Lindsay is now back at her school teaching music and loving it. Talk about strength of spirit and "rising" to the occasion.

Lindsay still struggles and grieves over her dreams of starting a family not coming to fruition yet. Infertility isn't a subject that is talked about much in society. People do not realize how hard Mother's Day can be. Comments like, "It just wasn't God's timing," after a miscarriage can hurt deeply. Lindsay recognizes that people just don't know what to say. Sometimes the best way to show love to someone is to say nothing, but support them with your physical presence. She loves her nieces and nephews, but her hopes and dreams were to have her own kids playing with their cousins. Facebook posts seem to announce almost daily that another one of her friends is expecting a baby in the months ahead. She feels guilty for not always feeling immediate joy for those friends.

Through it all, Lindsay wants to allow her brokenness to be a light for others. She wants to be able to open the conversation about infertility. It can be a very uncomfortable subject. Statistics and definitions don't begin to tap into the pain, disappointment, bitterness, and isolation of not being able to have a child. She wants to allow God to use her pain to help people understand that they have permission to voice their distress and despair. Working through those feelings is part of the process. It's also important to know that in God's plan, no pain is wasted. God is not finished, and He will continue to bring hope and a future.

Lindsay's beautiful voice continues to sing praises to God when she joins the worship band on frequent Sundays. It is not fake or hypocritical. She has come to a place with God that she believes she will be able to hold her own child someday. The emotional reality is still painfully overwhelming at times, much like the cries of Hannah in the Bible.

In 1 Samuel, we find Hannah weeping and praying to the Lord for a child. Her state of barrenness had her in a place of anguish and grief, pouring out her heart to God. Eli, the priest, saw her lips moving but no sound was heard. He mistakenly thought she was drunk. As he questioned Hannah, it became evident that she was praying. Eli blessed her, granted her peace, and said, "May the God of Israel grant you what you have asked of him" I Samuel 1:17.

I find it interesting that Hannah arose with her husband and worshiped the Lord the next morning. This was before there was any indication that Hannah's prayer for a child had been answered. The verse says that "in the course of time" Hannah conceived and gave birth to a son. We have no idea if it was immediately or years after her initial prayer. We do know that she went forward in faith, and God did grant her request.

Lindsay's story isn't over. She is clinging to God's promises to enable her to "rise." She has claimed Isaiah 66:9. As she chooses **higher ground**, it doesn't mean she can't or shouldn't grieve or continue to weep and pray. It just means she knows that God is waiting with her. She can talk to Him and seek His will for her life and future family. She can claim victory as she sings the lyrics from *Take Courage* by Bethel Music:

> So take courage my heart
> Stay steadfast my soul
> He's in the waiting
> He's in the waiting
> And hold onto your hope
> As your triumph unfolds
> He's never failing
> He's never failing
>
> And you who hold the stars
> Who call them each by name
> Will surely keep your promise to me
> That I will **RISE** in Your victory

Summing it Up:
- Blessing others means looking out for their interests above those of your own.
- A quick look at the Psalms reveals that David often spoke out in anger to God about his circumstances before moving forward in trust.
- Sometimes the best way to show love to someone is to say nothing, but support them with your physical presence.
- Hannah arose with her husband and worshiped the Lord before there was any physical indication that Hannah's prayer for a child had been answered.

☀ Highlights from God's Word:
- Philippians 2:4
- Psalm 4
- Job 2:13
- 1 Samuel 1:19-20

Memos of Mountaintop Moments

Chapter 23
SHOE GRACE

Blessed are the merciful for they will be shown mercy.
Matthew 5:7

The kids were so excited. It was the last hurrah of summer before school started. Grandma and Grandpa were picking up the four siblings for a day trip to the beach. The weather had consistently been in the triple digits in their hometown, so a cool ocean breeze and a chance to use their new boogie boards in the waves had everyone jumping in place as they anticipated being picked up.

The lunch was packed, the overnight bags were in the back of the car, and the swim gear was ready. The only thing left was to get the kids secured in their car seats and seatbelts. The older two were able to take care of themselves, but the younger two required a bit of assistance.

"Everybody set?" asked grandpa. The responses were all affirmative.

As the enthusiastic group settled in for the two-hour drive, grandma prayed for the Lord's blessing on their trip. The rules were reviewed, simply stated: get along, no whining, and stops will be made for whoever needs a break. With ages ranging from seven to thirteen, the importance of patience and cooperation needed to be highlighted and reaffirmed.

About thirty miles down the road, the opportunity to test the rules presented itself. The nine-year-old needed to use the restroom. Grandpa pulled into the first available minimart to allow for the needed relief. The seven-year-old decided he would "try," just to be on the safe side. The older two claimed to be fine.

As grandma opened the door to accompany her granddaughter inside, she noticed her granddaughter was about to hop out of the car shoeless. When told to put her shoes on, the granddaughter replied nonchalantly, "Oh, I don't need them."

"Oh, yes, you do. You can't walk into the store barefooted."

Her apparent indifference was really avoidance, and soon everyone realized her shoes had been left behind. She had been so excited when everyone piled in the car, she had buckled in without her flip-flops. Grandma ran into the minimart to see if they had some sandals or flip-flops for purchase on one of the display carousels. Nothing. It was determined that they would have to stop later down the road where there were other store options to pick up an inexpensive pair of shoes for her. In the meantime, she borrowed the oversized flip-flops of her older sister to take care of the immediate need.

The older two siblings were quite put off! They reprimanded their little sister, insisting that they had reminded her to put her shoes on as they were waiting for the ride to arrive. Rolling their eyes, they just couldn't believe she had forgotten. It was going to ruin the entire trip, they were certain.

Grandma reminded them of the patience part of the rules. It was the perfect moment to talk about grace. When someone has made a mistake or even completely blown it, we must give them the benefit of the doubt. The person who made the mistake usually feels terrible already. Piling more guilt upon them doesn't help matters. Where there's a problem, there is most likely always a solution.

The older two heeded the advice and cooled their jets. The stop for the "necessary" was completed and they were on their way once again. Several miles before the beach destination, the flip-flop purchase was made, and all was well. The beach day was fabulous. The waves were perfect. The sun was shining, and each child wore themselves out riding the surf for several hours.

After cleaning up at the hotel, everyone hungrily devoured a McDonald's dinner and had no problem falling asleep. The next morning, the plan was to have breakfast at one of the grandparents' favorite local cafes, take a walk along the beach front shops, and head back home. Since the restaurant was within walking distance, the party of six took off down the hill toward their breakfast destination.

Waffles and pancakes, orange juice and coffee, and eggs and bacon, graced the various table settings. The kids were filled and content and ready to get checked out of the hotel. On the way back up the hill, the oldest sibling tripped over an unseen crack in the sidewalk which caused her sandal to break. Without an extra pair of shoes, she would be unable to walk through the shops.

The decision was made to just skip that part of the plan and head on home. How ironic that the one who had to show "shoe" mercy and grace the day before was now the one needing to receive the mercy and grace from the others for herself. They all empathized, laughed a little at the shoe shenanigans that seemed to plague the trip, and finished packing the car to go home.

This is a simple illustration of what Jesus may have meant as He was teaching the sermon on the mount. If we show mercy, we will receive it when we most need it. It is so easy to be judgmental of the mistakes of others without looking inward at our own erroneous ways. We may ask, how could they do that? Why couldn't they have used more common sense or have seen the storm coming? We feel certain we would never make a mistake like that.

When Jesus was talking about judging others, He painted a great word picture. He first reminded us that we would be judged by the same measure as we judge others. Next, He said we should not work so hard at getting the speck out of our brother's or sister's eye when we have a plank in our own eye (see Matthew 7:3). It may cause a bit of a chuckle to visualize the person with the large board in their eye trying to worry about the speck of dust in the other person's eye. Whether it was supposed to be humorous or not, it's easy to see the point of His admonition.

Judging others is certainly something to work on, but sometimes, we have trouble giving grace to ourselves. We feel like our sin is too big to be forgiven. We may know God has forgiven us, but we are sure He won't be able to use someone with such a flawed past. We allow guilt to heap onto our hearts until it crushes our ability to see God's goodness. We are the ones holding onto our guilt and sin. God, on the other hand, once our sin is confessed before Him, removes our transgressions as far as the east is from the west (see Psalm 103:12).

I participate in an on-line Pilates class. The thirty-something mom of four who teaches the daily routines offers support and inspiration as you start your exercise journey with her. One of her catch phrases is "Grace over guilt." She encourages everyone to work according to their own pace and space in the exercise spectrum. She urges us to appropriately laugh at ourselves when trying, and failing, a new move or position. She promotes the idea for her audience to count progress over perfection. She consistently persuades us not to beat ourselves up over missing a day or getting off track for a season. She gently cheers us on to get back on the mat as soon as possible.

It's the same in Christ's kingdom. When we enter a relationship with Jesus by accepting his grace, we are not expected to pray perfectly, have no future faults, or know everything there is to know about our new life in Him. We have all fallen short, and we will continue to fail. If Christ hadn't given His life in substitution for the death that we deserve, we would not have any hope of eternal life. We have been saved by grace, not because of anything we have done (see Ephesians 2:8-9). His grace continues to extend to us, not so we have an excuse to live however we want, but so that we can "get back on the mat" and keep participating in all the benefits He has for us.

It's reassuring to know that our hard work isn't what is required to receive God's grace. If it depended on us, we would either be puffed up with pride or totally discouraged with failure. Instead, He offers grace over guilt, progress over perfection, as our avenue to **higher ground**. He knows we are going to forget our shoes someday, and He has "shoe grace" available for all who will receive it.

⤴ Summing it Up:

- If we show mercy, we will receive it when we most need it.
- It is so easy to be judgmental of the mistakes of others without looking inward to our own erroneous ways.
- We have all fallen short and need Christ's mercy and grace.
- . We are the ones holding onto our guilt and sin. God, on the other hand, once our sin is confessed before Him, removes our transgressions as far as the east is from the west.

☀ Highlights from God's Word:

- Matthew 5:7
- Matthew 7:3
- Romans 3:23; Ephesians 2:8-9
- Psalm 103:12

Memos of Mountaintop Moments

Chapter 24
THE BRIDE OF THE LAMB

For the wedding of the Lamb has come, and his bride has made herself ready. Fine linen, bright and clean, was given her to wear.
Revelation 19:7b-8

"You want me to do what?" Chris asked in disbelief.

"Come over and try on my wedding dress." Sarah repeated, as if it was an every-day request. This was not the first time Sarah had surprised Chris.

After twenty-two years of drug addiction, which included eleven prison stints, Chris had met the Lord in a miraculous encounter. Jesus freed her completely from the desires and behaviors of the past. He had given her peace and purpose. She had a growing hunger for reading and learning about what God's Word had to say.

Chris was making drastic changes to her lifestyle. Knowing that it was important to keep herself busy with positive activity and surrounding herself with like-minded people, Chris and her boyfriend, Harry, began attending the Saturday night service at Olive Knolls. Chris considered herself a misfit in this congregation of primarily middle-class Jesus-lovers. She knew she was redeemed, but she had such a stained past.

Sarah did not contemplate any differences when she spotted Chris across the foyer for the first time. Sarah made a beeline for Chris, introduced herself, and welcomed the newcomers. How dumbfounded Chris was that Sarah's welcoming greeting didn't stop there. It was more than just her greeters' duty. Sarah genuinely cared about people she welcomed, and she invited Chris and Harry into their home. Sarah lived out the fact that God does not show favoritism! The backgrounds of this new couple included a dramatic rescue from lives of destruction. Chris and Harry had been baptized into Christ, and had clothed themselves with Christ. The two couples were giving and receiving a blessed gift of friendship, love, and acceptance. They had so much to learn from each other, even though they weren't yet aware of the abundance of God's plan.

Sarah and Mike, her husband, volunteered to help Chris and Harry feed the homeless, a ministry that started from the compassion they felt over those who were in situations similar to what they had lived previously. This bonding through acts of service created a unity in Christ and a deepening of their relationship. Sarah was the first "healthy" friend that Chris had ever had—Sarah was someone who didn't selfishly want anything from her. She was someone who made her feel comfortable and loved.

Over time the leadership at Olive Knolls began to gently encourage Chris and Harry to get married. They very much wanted to obey Christ's teachings and properly unite, but Chris wanted a special wedding, something she had never had in her previous lifestyle. They were waiting because of the expense. Then, the idea began to develop. Why not get married at a Saturday night service? The close community of friends they had developed would be present. One of the attendees did photography. Someone else knew how to arrange flowers. Another could provide a cake for a reception. The pastor already knew their story and loved them. But there was the issue of a dress.

That's when Sarah felt led to unseal her wedding dress and loan it to Chris. It might just fit. They had similar body styles. Besides, what good was it sitting unused in a closet? So here Chris was, trying it on, five and a half years after Sarah had worn it down a wedding aisle. It fit perfectly! She had never felt so beautiful. Sarah took pictures to send to Chris's mom. Tears of joy streamed down their faces.

The wedding was beautiful. It preceded the worship service, and the evening flowed together impeccably. It went beyond Chris's expectations. She had never felt so loved. God used the body of believers to build her and Harry up in His power, and they both were finding it hard to grasp how high and deep God's love was for them. We can never underestimate what it is God can do in and through us to show His boundless riches.

This was only the beginning. The unlikely friendship of Sarah and Chris was God-created. Though the world would have never put them together, God brought them to His **higher ground** of acceptance and mutual give-and-take. It wouldn't be too far in the future before Sarah would need to rely on Chris for some crucial life issues.

Sarah had grown up in a Christian home. One of the things that made a lasting impression on her and her brothers and sisters was when her parents adopted some younger siblings. It changed their life perspectives and gave them a heart for the hurting and broken. Over time, Sarah and Mike began to talk about adopting some of their own. After giving birth to two healthy boys, they felt God was preparing them to take the next step.

They thought, at first, they would be adopting babies from Ethiopia. That door was providentially closed, and eventually the plan changed. One Easter Sunday while sitting in church, watching all the little girls in their bows and pretty dresses, Sarah found herself weeping inexplicably. At that moment she felt an assurance that God was preparing two girls for them. Not long after that Sunday morning, an opportunity presented itself to adopt four and six-year-old sisters who were in the foster care system. Their family increased to four kids overnight through a series of God-ordained circumstances.

Chris and Harry continued to be a part of their lives, even more so now that they had increased their family size. They would join the family for cookie decorating. They ate dinners together. They even vacationed together a few times. These activities filled a void in Chris's life that she had missed when she was living for herself. She had six children of her own who had been adopted out or removed from her because of her addictions. Spending time with these new friends and their family brought healing.

Through the course of the next several years, Mike and Sarah adopted subsequent siblings of the girls. It was important to them that the brothers and sisters have contact and connection with each other. They now have nine kids total. They need a fifteen-passenger van to transport everyone at one time, and a motorhome is reserved for longer trips and vacations. There are difficult adjustments as the children transition from their former places of dysfunction. There are medical issues—mental, emotional, and physical. The road hasn't always been easy, and not everyone is understanding or tolerant of the chaos that sometimes ensues with that many kids navigating through life, much less a store or church foyer. But Chris and Harry have never blinked an eye or had a critical word to offer.

When it became clear that Sarah could use some extra help, she asked if Chris would be willing to be hired to clean house once a week. This deepened their relationship. When she came, Chris would do the prescribed cleaning, but she also changed a diaper when it was needed or took the kids to the park for a few minutes to give Sarah a break. The best thing that happened was the deep conversations the two women began to have. Friendships (likely and unlikely) can open our hearts to things we might never have considered before. It is one of the ways that enables God to do immeasurably more than all we ask or imagine.

Chris could give credence and understanding to why the kids' mom would continue to get pregnant, only to have to give up her baby. She had been in the mom's shoes herself. She helped explain how an addict always thought that this time, this pregnancy, it would be different. She articulated the love that the birth mom had for her children, even when it wasn't evident to the on-lookers. Chris was a safe friend who could enter into the commotion of this busy home with no judgment, just help and empathy. The honesty and vulnerability of the two women cultivated a deep abiding friendship. Chris helped Sarah not only gain a new appreciation for what her children were going through, but she obtained greater insight in how to pray for the kids' mom.

In a recent video testimony that Chris gave for a Sunday morning church service, she ended by talking about how she sees miracles every day. It might just be that you wake up breathing in the morning. It might be seeing a life changed and transformed by the love of Jesus. She encouraged the listeners to know that God is always there and that praying is enough.

One of the biggest miracles for Chris was her friendship with Sarah. Wearing her friend's wedding dress had been more than she could have ever thought or imagined. Chris was a beautiful bride on that day, in every sense, physically and spiritually. In her prison cell, Chris had prayed and submitted her life to Jesus. He gave her fine linen, bright and clean, to wear, and she is a living testimony of becoming the bride of Christ.

Summing it Up:
- God does not show favoritism!
- God uses the body of believers to build us up in His power and to grasp how high and deep His love is.
- Friendships (likely and unlikely) can open our hearts to things we might never have considered before. It is one of the ways that enables God to do immeasurably more than all we ask or imagine.
- We are living testimonies of being the bride of Christ.

Highlights from God's Word:
- Acts 10:34; Galatians 3:26-29
- Ephesians 3:17-19
- Ephesians 3:20
- Revelation 19:7b-8

Memos of Mountaintop Moments

Chapter 25
TRAIN UP A CHILD

Train a child in the way he should go, and when he is old he will not turn from it. Proverbs 22:6

My sister-in-law, Cathy, is a retired children's pastor. She has a great heart for kids, and she ran an amazing program for hundreds of children during her years at Bend Nazarene Church. Maybe that is why she was so disheartened when she couldn't find a Vacation Bible School happening during the summer of 2020. Churches were going on-line and camps and kids' activities were being canceled in lieu of safety and trying to quell the pandemic.

The idea began to brew, and Cathy decided to conduct a small neighborhood VBS (Vacation Bible School). She was able to garner the help of a couple of her good friends. Denise would organize water games since she was the "queen of outdoor games." Sheri would be the ultimate helper for all the activities, an aide-de-camp to Cathy for all things VBS. They planned Bible stories, songs, crafts, and snacks. Even Cathy's husband, Don, got in on an object lesson by teaching the kids how to make paper airplanes. Cathy's four grandkids and about six neighborhood children became the intimate little group to learn about Jesus on Monday, Wednesday, and Friday, from 9:00-11:00 a.m.

When asked about her motivation for putting this together, Cathy said, "I just felt like the kids were missing out on Christian Ed[ucation] because of Covid. It is so important to feed their little hearts." With songs and motions in their memory banks, powerful stories from the Bible, and the crafts and activities that continued to hone in on the lessons being taught, Cathy found it a great way to connect. The theme throughout the week was "Jesus gives me the power…" The children explored how Jesus gives them the power to go through hard times, and they could definitely put that into practice as they maneuvered through the pandemic with the rest of the community. They learned that Jesus gives them the power to be a friend.

They ended the week with a rock painting activity. They wrote the words "Be a friend" on their rocks and were given the task to "plant" it somewhere away from their home or neighborhood. They were excited about the prospect of someone picking it up and being encouraged to be someone's friend.

It took some planning and the sacrifice of a few summer mornings, but Cathy resolved to do it again. We cannot diminish the power of planting the seed of God's Word in our children's hearts. The Bible promises that when we train a child in the way of wisdom, he or she will always fall back on it (see Proverbs 22:6). During His ministry, Jesus showed love to the little children. Their innocence and transparency were probably very refreshing to Him compared to the arrogance and hypocrisy of some of the religious leaders He was dealing with. The harvest is ripe with hearts that are hungering to connect with the God of the Universe, and our children often lead the way.

It was some of these thoughts that influenced my husband and I as August 2020 and the new school year was approaching. "Certainly, the schools would reopen in the fall," we had thought. We had helped out our oldest son and wife by taking the kids during the last couple of months in the spring when schools closed due to the Covid-19 pandemic. We were retired and looking forward to an uneventful fall. Our plans took a drastic turn (see more details in Chapter 21). As the first day of school arrived, we were privileged to have the kids begin the school year with us. The first thing we recognized that we needed to do was to call our Internet provider to up our bandwidth. We needed the capacity to handle four computers on Zoom each day.

By 7:10 a.m. each morning the four munchkins, ages 12, 10, 8, and 6, would arrive. Their Zoom classrooms started sometime between 8:00 and 8:30 a.m., depending on the student and their school schedule. The first few mornings were a little chaotic. We quickly realized that we needed some type of structure to keep them from bickering or running amok.

We conducted a family meeting in which we explained the routine for the morning. They would come in, put their lunches away, fill their water bottles, set up their work stations, and then we would meet in the family room for devotions. We started going through the gospel of Matthew, reading and discussing the stories about Jesus. Eventually I purchased a kids' devotional book, and the kids took turns reading the scripture and lesson. We always ended with prayer requests, and each child prayed for one or more of the requests.

Several things stood out to me during that time. We were honored to get a peek into their hearts. Some of the discussion, questions, and prayers were so profound. It started our day off so well. The Word of God was being planted in their minds and souls, and we could remind them throughout the week of what we had read or talked about. Their training went beyond books and videos or pen and paper. It was establishing God's Word in their hearts.

Years ago, there was a young couple who also believed in the power of training children in the ways of Jesus. If you drive by a small plot of property on Lucille Avenue in Bakersfield, California, you might not even notice what is there. It looks like it could be a shed or a small barn. The red planks and white window shutters have faded with time. It sits empty on its grassy parcel, its windows boarded up and its door locked. If this small 14-by-17-foot inanimate building could speak, it would have much to say about what transpired behind its walls just a few decades ago. It was a place of **higher ground** for neighborhood children to learn about the Savior who loved them unconditionally and with open hearts.

In the mid 1960's, a Bakersfield couple, Bill and Eunice Carter, began to feel a tug on their heart for the children around their housing development. Each Sunday morning as they were driving to church, they would see many of these kids playing with their friends. Their van, housing their own family of five, would often transport a few other children to Sunday School, but there were far too many being left behind.

During a family vacation, the Carters saw the children's chapel in Storybook Land at the Fresno Zoo. When they came home, they started building their own version of a children's church on the property they owned adjacent to their home. The neighborhood kids assisted with the project. Mr. Carter took personal care as he made wooden pews for the children to sit on. The windows were crafted with long, lean panes of glass that let just the right amount of sunlight in. The walls were graced with pictures of Jesus, and many portrayed little children all around Him.

It was more than a playhouse or kids' structure. It was a special place of worship, and once it was built, it didn't take long to fill it each Sunday morning. Kids brought their friends and siblings, until the inside was brimming with squirming, excited, balls of energy.

On any given Sunday, there would be upwards of sixty plus students joining the Carters in singing songs, such as "Only a Boy Named David," with motions included. They would pray and take an offering, only because the children wanted to contribute, but never a request or requirement by the Carters. The offerings were sent to missionaries who would send back thank you notes, sharing what their money had helped to accomplish. A flannel board was used to display characters and background scenes that helped illustrate the Bible stories.

The Carter family all pitched in. Their oldest daughter, thirteen years old, played the piano during the song time. Their eleven-year-old son was the treasurer and custodian, and sometimes played the guitar. The youngest daughter helped round up the neighborhood kids when it was about time to start. Mrs. Carter would fix sandwiches and serve the students lunch before sending them home. It was truly a family affair.

One of the beneficiaries of this chapel was my friend Shari. She was the one who brought the story to my attention. When she was nine, Shari lived in a dysfunctional home. Her mom worked long hours trying to make ends meet after a divorce. Shari's older brothers were often in trouble, and her home was not always a place of peace. The children's chapel each Sunday morning was her safe haven.

The songs and stories filled Shari's soul in a way she couldn't really describe. She does remember that on one occasion, when an invitation was extended to ask for forgiveness and give her heart to the Lord, Shari raised her hand and prayed the sinner's prayer. She began a relationship with Jesus that day. Though she walked away for a time during young adulthood, Shari now reflects on how much she has counted on her relationship with Jesus and studying His Word, the Bible.

Shari recently had lunch with one of her childhood friends, also named Sheri. Sheri recalled being incentivized to memorize and recite Bible verses in order to "earn" their very OWN Bible. Sheri still has her Bible and several religious bookmarks that she earned. The black leather Bible has her name inscribed in gold. Inside, written in cursive, it says presented to Sharon G., awarded by Children's Church, 4-4-69. This gift provides a priceless memory and an ongoing legacy for Sheri and the other children who worked for it.

From these early years, Shari learned the value and importance of fellowship. She loved playing with her friends. They would break into small groups on the grassy area in front of the chapel to get a little more individualized attention. At the time, there was a college student and a high school girl who would help with the teaching and managing of all the kids. They were given the opportunity to play together and eat together, always being shown the utmost care and respect.

The Carters also began an adult Bible study on Wednesday nights. The adults would gather in the living room while the kids played in another room and occasionally did a craft or organized activity. Shari's mom attended that Bible study and grew in her commitment to Christ as well. During one of the Wednesday nights when Shari was ten years old, she and her friends made little cards about their best friend. Shari had kept her card, decorated with stickers and felt markers. It said:

> "My best friend is God. God is the best friend anybody could have. God is friendship and happiness. God is Nature. But best of all is receiving God into your heart. God is LOVE!"

The Carters were models of God's love. There are probably many stories from the kids who lived around the Lucille neighborhood Children's Church and benefited from the mentoring and love of this family. So many homes then, as now, were full of their own dysfunction and problems. The Carters provided a place of learning, safety, play and prayer.

The Carters would most likely be the first to say that they weren't perfect, but they were willing to be used by God. A newspaper article in 2005 pictured the couple celebrating their 55th wedding anniversary. They were being congratulated by their three children, eight grandchildren, four great grandchildren, and a multitude of friends. One of the reasons for their successful years of marriage was they agreed to live their lives with the Lord sharing an equal part in their marriage. The newspaper anniversary announcement stated that through many blessings and trials, their faith has been secure. God is faithful.

When interviewed for an earlier article about the chapel in the local paper in 1968, Mr. Carter said, "Maybe if one person's heart is right, that can spread throughout the neighborhood and continue throughout the United States. Maybe it can mean a better country.

You can't expect the politicians to straighten out the hate in our hearts. We have an obligation to help our neighbor. It's one of the Ten Commandments—Love Thy Neighbor as Thyself, but it's hard [to love] if you don't know Him."

His prophetic statement was no truer in 1968 than it is today. We do have an obligation to love our neighbors. I have been convicted through this story about the neighborhood kids on our street who are inside their homes or outside playing each Sunday morning. The parents and friends that we see occasionally when we are out in front of our homes are hungry for God's Word, even though they may not recognize it. May we listen to God's voice to move our love into action.

Summing it Up:

- We cannot diminish the power of planting the seed of God's Word in our children's hearts.
- Jesus loves little children, and He invites them to come to Him.
- The harvest is ripe for those who need to hear about the love of Jesus.
- We can show others God's unconditional love by modeling that love.
- It's hard to love your neighbor as yourself if you don't know Him. God is love!

☀ Highlights from God's Word:
- Proverbs 22:6
- Mark 10:13-16
- Matthew 9:37-38
- 1 John 3:16
- Mark 12:30-31; 1 John 4:16

Memos of Mountaintop Moments

Chapter 26
SEEING THE GOD WHO SEES

She gave this name to the Lord who spoke to her: "You are the God who sees me," for she said, "I have now seen the One who sees me." Genesis 16:13

One of the most compelling stories in the Old Testament is found in Genesis 16. Abram and Sarai were well past their years of bearing children. Sarai, who was obviously and painfully barren, decided to take matters into her own hands. In a discussion with Abram, she shared her brilliant idea to start their family through her maidservant, Hagar. Abram agreed, and soon Hagar was pregnant.

The whirlpool of emotions began. Hagar, feeling used by her masters, began to despise her mistress. Sarai blamed Abram. Abram gave Sarai permission to "do with [Hagar] whatever you think best," and Sarai began to mistreat Hagar. Now Hagar could list an entourage of additional emotions: abused, betrayed, oppressed, diminished, rejected, and unwanted. She fled from the situation, adding "unprotected" to her arsenal of reactions, compounded by the pregnancy hormones that were most likely raging.

Here is the amazing part of this story. God pursued Hagar in the desert where she had stopped by a spring, exhausted and thirsty. He spoke to her and listened to her reply. God then instructed her to return to her mistress, but He promised to bless her. Now came the pivotal moment. Hagar had the choice to reject God's call on her life and continue on her own path, or she could follow God's direction, even though it meant returning to her place of pain.

Hagar's response is one that touches all of us. She gave God the name "You are the God who sees me." She knew that returning would not be easy, but she was willing to go where God was calling her so that she could learn of His goodness and receive His blessing. Her story illustrates that God loves, pursues, comforts, and sustains us through our pain. We want to see immediate results, to be removed from our situation, or have the problem taken from us, but that just might keep us from seeing the God who sees us.

I met a modern-day Hagar at a Market Place event where vendors were selling their homemade and original wares. I had a book table. Trina had a table filled with handmade crosses, bookmarks, and jewelry. During a lull in business, I visited her table. She came by my table later in the day. Trina's business is called "Glory for Jesus." Her business card has a picture of a cross inside a teardrop, set in a blue sky above silver-lined clouds. This logo is a perfect depiction of the **higher ground** that Trina has chosen.

Trina exuded the joy and exuberance that could only come from a redeemed life. There wasn't always joy in her life. In fact, Trina was mistreated by those closest to her for a large portion of her life. She felt:

- Unprotected
- Unwanted
- Neglected

- Abused
- Rejected
- Abandoned
- Invisible

Trina has early childhood memories of weekend parties in her home where she would receive no attention from Friday to Monday. She would not be fed or bathed. There would be no bed-time story or being tucked into her covers. When the weekdays started again, Trina would head off to school, knowing that another weekend was looming in the near future.

To compound the problems, Trina had trouble learning. She had problems reading and writing. Her teachers didn't give her learning disabilities any close attention, and she was passed from grade to grade with the problems getting worse each year. Without her family advocating for her, there didn't seem to be any solution.

One Friday night, with the backdrop of blaring music, people drunk and high all over the house, ten-year-old Trina decided it was time to leave this world. She found her mom's sleeping pills in the medicine cabinet and took the entire bottle. The next morning, to her dismay, Trina woke up. She could not control her vomiting, which was surely what saved her life, as her body rejected the effects of the drugs she had consumed. No one in the household was even aware of her dilemma.

Trina usually walked to church on Sundays with a friend, so she knew about God. She prayed to Him and tried to make sense of her circumstances. She now concluded, in her young mind, that since God didn't let her come to Heaven through her attempt at death,

God must not want her either. She felt totally rejected by her family, teachers, and God.

Life continued to get tougher. Trina experienced physical, verbal, and emotional abuse daily. One day, in her junior year of high school, Trina came home to a volatile situation. Her brother was upset and took it out on her physically. Her mother saw what was happening, but she did nothing to stop it. When the police finally came, her mother chose her brother over her, and Trina was forced to leave her home.

Eventually Trina got married, and over time her husband began to shower her with abuse. He would kick her in the head or back, places where the bruises and evidence of harm would not be visible to the outsider. When Trina finally had the courage to stand up for herself, she ended the relationship and sent him away.

Free from the grips of her tyrant husband, Trina began to attend church and Bible studies once again. She met a man named Tony, who was a man of God, her angel, as she calls him. Tony and Trina dated for three years, and they were married in 1996. Finally, she had a man who treated her as she deserved. He loved her and took care of her needs. For the first time in her life, she knew she was not invisible. She was seen by God, and she began to see and believe that God had a plan for her life.

With the help of her new husband, Trina and Tony poured themselves into raising her grandson, Raymond. When Raymond came to live with them permanently, at the age of two, he had to be nursed back to health. His lungs had been severely damaged due to living in a house filled with meth and marijuana. Once Raymond was healthy enough, Trina got him into Head Start. For a while

Trina worked at the same preschool. She had such compassion for the little ones who were behind in their academic abilities. She worked especially hard with those students who struggled, and she created a curriculum for them that would help them get a boost before they entered elementary school. She did not want ANYONE to feel like she had felt as a child: forgotten, left behind, invisible.

When she could no longer work in this capacity because of residual back pain and brain injuries from previous abuses, Trina began her business. She is not totally pain free, but Trina is a walking miracle. She is able to look back at how God preserved her life so that He could eventually lead her into a place of peace and joy, freedom in salvation, purpose, and blessings beyond comprehension. She now knows that God saw her all along, and He was preparing her to see the little ones who would be brought into her path.

We all find ourselves in the character of Hagar or Trina. Whether it is a lifetime of abuse or a season of feeling unloved and misunderstood, God wants you to know that He sees you. In a recent Proverbs 31 Ministry podcast, guest Kia Stephens laid out "Five Truths About God's Love for Us." She reminded us through the story of Hagar that:
1. We are noticed by God. He finds you through relentless pursuit.
2. We are heard by God. He wants you to wrestle through your thoughts and hurts.
3. We are blessed by God. He will sustain you right where you are.
4. We are restored by God. He will bring about His purpose in your life as you learn to wait with Him through the process.

5. We are seen by God. He is concerned about you, and He loves you.[7]

The higher path is not always the easy path. Trina would attest to that! God's purpose is sometimes seen as we look back and see how He used our past pain for present good. All along the way, you are seen and loved by God. Allow Him to show you His love and you will see the God who sees.

↑ Summing it Up:

- We want to see immediate results, to be removed from our situation, or have the problem taken from us, but that just might keep us from seeing the God who sees us.
- She worked especially hard with those students who struggled, and she created a curriculum for them that would help them get a boost before they entered elementary school. She did not want ANYONE to feel like she had felt as a child: forgotten, left behind, invisible.
- God preserves your life so that He can eventually lead you into a place of peace and joy, freedom in salvation, purpose, and blessings beyond comprehension.
- The higher path is not always the easy path. God's purpose is sometimes seen as we look back and see how He used our past pain for present good.

☀ Highlights from God's Word:

- Genesis 16:7-13
- 2 Corinthians 1:3-4

---

[7] Brock, Meredith (Host). (2020, June 2). *5 Truths About God's Love For Us* [Audio podcast]. The Proverbs 31 Ministries Podcast. https://proverbs31.org/listen/podcast/full-podcast/2020/06/02/5-truths-about-god's-love-for-us

- Psalm 16:9-11
- Hebrews 12:11

Memos of Mountaintop Moments

Chapter 27
LORD, GIVE ME STRENGTH

I can do everything through him who gives me strength.
Philippians 4:13

Chris Schwartz is familiar with change. He has understood throughout his life that he must rely on God for his strength so that he can manage new circumstances.

A major change he recently went through was a career change. After years of working as a Senior Emergency Preparedness Coordinator, Chris changed to a profession in teaching. Chris has always been great with kids, and this was a natural fit in so many ways. The strength God gave him as he and his wife, Robin, shifted their finances and acclimated to his schedule of taking university classes, studying for qualifying tests, and seeking job placement was evident daily.

Chris chuckled as he looked back on the five years he has been head of a classroom of students. The first year was...the first year. As is the case for all new teachers, it was a year of learning and adjustments. His second year was plagued with a partner teacher that was removed from her classroom mid-year. There was also the frustration of multiple attempts at passing the RICA, a series of three subtests that are part of the credentialing process. His third year was at a new school. Midway through the first semester, the district experienced a ransomware attack and had to revert to keeping all of their grades and documentation by pen and paper. Toward the end of that school year, in March 2020, the schools were closed and Zoom teaching was assumed because of a pandemic known as the coronavirus.

The fourth year, fall of 2020, began with Zoom classrooms on steroids. The challenge was to keep high expectations, but the reality of connecting with students solely on line was elusive. Students were finally admitted back into the classroom shortly after the first of the year in 2021, but everyone was a bit behind. Kids who were used to being at home each day for their lessons had to readjust to life in a classroom with masks, plexiglass shields, and alternating schedules so that everyone could stay distanced and safe.

Looking forward to his fifth year being a little bit more normal, Chris was optimistic. Unfortunately, a summer road trip, sitting too long for extended periods of time in his truck, had created severe back pain. His doctor found that he had a 50% fracture in his vertebra. He couldn't pinpoint the cause of the fracture, but he recommended a procedure called vertebroplasty, in which the fractures would be filled with a cement-like substance to relieve pain and restore mobility.

That was not going to stop Chris from going to class every day. He would tough it out until the procedure was scheduled. Before he could even get to that point, Chris found himself at the urgent care on a late September weekend with severe sinus issues. He figured it was a sinus infection, but he ended up testing positive for Covid-19. He had to follow the school district's protocol of staying home until his symptoms were gone and he had a negative test.

Since he had been vaccinated, Chris figured he would ride it out with mild symptoms. By Thursday, Robin knew "mild" was not the case. Things had turned serious. His trouble breathing and lack of energy and mental acuity made her realize that she needed to get him to the hospital immediately. It took Chris two hours just to get ready to go to the emergency room. He kept falling asleep in between the steps of getting ready, but they were finally out the door.

Robin dropped Chris off at the emergency room doors, and due to Covid-19 restrictions she was forced to wait outside in her parked car. Chris endured the normal ER processes, and ended up in a room, sectioned off by plastic sheets. The attending physician ran several tests and ordered him to be admitted to a hospital room. His kidneys were functioning at fourteen, with sixty to seventy being normal. The doctor said if he'd waited another twenty-four to forty-eight hours at home, he would have been dead. God's timing was amazing. Chris credits God and Robin for saving his life.

Chris stayed in the hospital for twelve more days. He had many tests, including a kidney ultrasound. He was given breathing treatments every few hours for the pneumonia in both lungs. Blood thinners were administered to keep his body stable throughout the various treatments. He was poked and prodded throughout all hours of the day and night. Hospitals are not the best places to get rest!

Robin quickly realized that she needed to be able to listen in when the doctors came by with results. Chris just wasn't processing it all, and he couldn't recall what they had said after they left. Robin started talking to the doctors and getting the reports as well. Again, it became apparent that God's perfect timing and plan was being executed. The attending ER physician had expressed concern about Chris's hands shaking. The tremor, Chris explained, was a familial trait. The doctor didn't buy it.

He came by Chris's room and ordered a CT scan of the brain. The scan revealed that three to four lesions were attached to Chris's skull. He advised Chris and Robin to follow up with an MRI when he left the hospital. Why was this particular doctor there that particular day when Chris went into the ER? Why would he not just let the explanation of family history be enough? God was true to who He is. He takes care of us, and our problems often end up being part of a much bigger picture to bring good out of our circumstances (Romans 8:28). Chris credits God and this doctor for giving him a second chance at life.

Chris was finally released on the same day that their daughter was giving birth to their granddaughter. Enjoying this blessing was put on hold while Chris had to spend two weeks at home, continuing physical therapy. Chris also set up an appointment for the MRI. On the day of the procedure, Robin again waited patiently in the car in the parking lot. (Oh, the Covid restrictions!) After the MRI was completed, the technician asked Chris if his wife was here. The doctor wanted to speak to them both.

Robin was let in. The news was grim. The doctor confirmed there were four to five lesions on the skull. He wanted to do a CT scan from the neck to the pelvis. There was an opening in the schedule, so they did it right then. The results showed another lesion on the L3 vertebra, and one on his right rib cage. It was recommended that they make an appointment with the local Comprehensive Blood and Cancer Center (CBCC) as soon as possible.

They had to wait for two weeks to see someone at CBCC, but again God's perfect plan was in place. The doctor they were assigned, Dr. Cartmell, was a believer in Jesus. He treated Chris like he was his only patient. He laid out what the possibilities were, but wanted to run a few more tests. When the test results came back, the doctor told Chris and Robin that he had early signs of multiple myeloma, a cancer of the plasma cells. They were finding it very early, so he wanted a bone marrow biopsy done to confirm the diagnosis.

The biopsy showed that the cancer was in his bone marrow. Treatment protocol was going to need to be discussed, but the prognosis was encouraging. It was all a waiting game at this point. Waiting for appointments, waiting for each doctor to determine the best timing and regimen. In the meantime, Chris went back to work. He needed his kids. Surprisingly, his back pain had subsided tremendously. The weeks of bedrest had allowed it to recover, and now they were pretty sure they knew what had caused the pain in the first place.

At the time of this writing, Chris just finished his first of five chemo treatments. When he finishes these treatments, he will head down to the City of Hope to receive a bone marrow transplant. Recovery will be slow, but he is encouraged by the recovery rates of other patients who have been through this process. His cancer will never go away completely, unless God chooses to intervene fully, and we know He can. It will be reduced greatly and monitored closely. If and when the cancer levels rise above a certain point, it will be treated with additional rounds of chemo.

Chris was overwhelmed with emotion as he pondered the goodness of God. He said, "God is going to protect. He's got a plan. I don't know what it is, but it's in His hands." If just one thing or person had been taken out of the equation, things could be so different.

Chris and Robin have also been so blessed by the prayers of many. Chris's nine-year-old grandson, visiting from North Dakota, prayed over his grandpa before heading back home. An acquaintance that brought back a borrowed trailer asked if he could pray with Chris. Their life group, their Bible studies, their pastors, family and friends, are all lifting his cancer and treatments to the Lord. The prayers of God's people are precious in God's sight.

Chris continues to teach school, lead a Sunday school class each Sunday, and he is working on his pastor's license. God is continuing to work out His plan and purpose for Chris's life. What Satan may have intended to bring discouragement and doubt, God is using for good. Chris knows that he couldn't do any of this without the strength of the Lord. He lives on **higher ground** as he leans daily on the promise of Philippians 4:13, "I can do everything through him who gives me strength."

SUMMING IT UP:

- Throughout our lives we must rely on God for our strength so that we can manage new circumstances that may come our way.
- God's timing is always perfect. We must acknowledge His ways and not lean on our own understanding.
- God is true to who He is. He takes care of us, and what seems like problems are so often part of a much bigger picture to bring good out of our circumstances.
- The prayers of God's people are precious in God's sight.
- What Satan may have intended to bring discouragement and doubt, God is using for good.

☀ HIGHLIGHTS FROM GOD'S WORD:
- Philippians 4:13
- Proverbs 3:5-6
- Romans 8:28
- James 5:16
- Genesis 50:20

Memos of Mountaintop Moments

Chapter 28
LOST AND FOUND

...he was lost and is found. So they began to celebrate.
Luke 15:24b

She didn't exactly *lose* her devices, but she definitely lost her feeling of connectivity. While on vacation, my eighty-eight-years-young mom inadvertently dropped her cell phone into a porcelain bowl of water. Somehow it had wedged its way out of her back pocket at a very inopportune moment! Regardless, it was rendered useless. We did all the things the Internet told us to do. We placed it in a bag of rice. We put it in a warm place. Since we were unable to remove the battery, the power remained on until it shorted out the system.

We even took it to a store called Ubreakifix. The technician was very kind as he told us that one of the worst things to do is put it in rice. He was able to remove the battery, along with a few grains of rice that had made their way into the crevices of the phone's innards. Upon drying everything out thoroughly, he let us know there was no hope for her phone.

No worries! She still had her iPad. This meant she could get emails and some texts. She could access her flight schedules and confirmation numbers. She could still feel connected to people through her Facebook account. She could take pictures to record her adventures, and she had her photo albums to show to the relatives she was visiting.

Everything seemed fine until she accidentally left her iPad behind at one of said relative's homes. Hours down the road, she realized it was missing. Too late to turn around, she berated herself for losing yet another means of communication and connection, just days apart, on the very same trip. After a few phone calls and a few too many pennies, it was arranged for the iPad to be sent via overnight delivery. When she met up with her lost gadget, there was celebration all around.

In a recent sermon on the lost and found of Luke 15, the pastor had researched the top five most commonly lost items. They were, in no particular order: phone, TV remote, keys, glasses, and wallet. When he listed these things, I was reminded of a ditty my son taught us last year. This song is to be sung to yourself as you are leaving your house to go somewhere or before getting in the car to return home. Using the tune to the preschool song, "Head and Shoulders, Knees and Toes," you replace the words with, "Glasses, wallet, keys, and phone..." (I can hear you trying it right now!). We laugh, but it works. These most essential things are the things we tend to lose or forget most often.

I have prayed many prayers to find my sunglasses or my keys. I have had people call my phone, only to locate it in the bottom of my purse or in my back pocket. I suspect that God has a sense of humor about these things, but He also understands their importance to us. We have had many celebrations when we find our lost items wedged between the couch cushions or even in the trash can.

My cousin, Sandy, shared a story about losing her ATM card (not in the top five, but it certainly should be in the top ten). She had been on a walk around her neighborhood. It must have flipped out of her pocket. When she realized it was gone, she retraced her steps, but to no avail. Before she had time to take care of canceling the card and procuring another, before she even left for work that morning, there was a knock at the door. An elderly man named Bill, aided by a walker, stood at the door returning her lost item.

Of course, there was celebration and heartfelt gratitude extended, but it didn't end there. Sandy was so impressed with this gentleman's kindness and honesty. It was even more impressive that he had researched where she lived and walked a one-and-a-half-mile round trip to return the card, with his walker. It was a sacrifice of care and giving. Sandy wanted to do more for Bill than just thank him.

As she planned how she could reciprocate her love and thanks, she found out a little more about Bill and his wife, Michiko. Michiko was from Japan. Sandy and her husband had worked in Japan for eleven years, so there was an immediate connection. Over time, a relationship was built with this couple. They shared a meal or two, exchanged a gift or two, and Sandy was able to assist them with moving some larger furniture items by enlisting the help of some of the young adults at her church.

The lost was found, but so much more than a bank card was gained that day. That is the **higher ground** economy of God's lost and found. When Jesus told the parables of the lost coin, sheep, and son, He was emphasizing the importance of a lost soul being welcomed into His kingdom. I have always felt that the greater miracles are not healings and big answers to prayer. The transformation of a life is so miraculous and great, that it is the only time where it is recorded that the angels throw a big party in Heaven. When a sinner comes to know Jesus, there is reason to celebrate!

With the permission of Pastor Brent Kall, discipleship and small group pastor at Olive Knolls Church, I want to share some of the points of his sermon on the parables of the lost.

First, he explained, we have the lost coin. The coin represents those people who are lost, but they don't know they are lost. They are oblivious and unaware that there's a God or a better way. They might think that their acts of righteousness have given them a standing with God. They need someone to search for them.

The lost sheep, Pastor Brent said, represent those who know they are lost, but they don't know how to get found. They are bewildered and disoriented. They don't know how to get "unlost." They need someone to seek them.

Finally, we were taught, the lost son represents those who are willfully resistant and rebellious. They know how to be found, but they are choosing to remain lost. They need someone who is persistent and patient in pursuing them.

All of the lost people matter to Jesus. They need to matter to us as well. If Jesus had not received and welcomed sinners (see Romans 5:8), He would not have received me and you. We need to be willing to search, seek, and pursue those who are lost. We must be willing to extend the same grace, kindness, forgiveness, and love that was shown to us.

Jesus modeled how to do this. He received the lost. He welcomed them. He ate meals with them. He found common ground and built relationships, because He wanted them to know they matter to

Him. In this context, His invitation for them to receive Jesus made sense and was often accepted.

We do not "save" others, but Jesus has given us the ultimate privilege and responsibility on this earth to reach out and share the gospel with others (Acts 1:8). We can do this best by displaying a welcoming spirit. We need to accept people into our lives and be willing to enter into their lives as well. They should know that every relationship is important. They should perceive that they matter to us.

When we show genuine love and grace, they are more likely to be open to God's voice. Those who don't know how to get found will be asking, "What do you have? What do I do to get some of that?" Those who don't know they are lost will begin to see that they are missing something. Those who have walked away from what they know is right will be more and more receptive to the love and grace being extended.

Then the party and celebration can begin. Yes, my mom was so grateful for getting her iPad back. Eventually, back at home, she ordered a new phone, and most of the data was restored. My cousin was thrilled to get back her bank card. I am equally grateful and ecstatic when I retrieve something that was momentarily lost or misplaced.

But these are merely things. When a life is restored, when a person who is lost is found, that is worth celebrating. Let the party begin!

SUMMING IT UP:

- Those who are lost need someone to search for them, seek after them, and extend love and grace to lead them back to Jesus.
- All of the lost people matter to Jesus. They need to matter to us as well. If Jesus had not received and welcomed sinners, He would not have received me and you.
- We do not "save" others, but Jesus has given us the ultimate privilege and responsibility on this earth to reach out and share the gospel with others.
- When a life is restored, when a person who is lost is found, that is worth celebrating. Let the party begin!

HIGHLIGHTS FROM GOD'S WORD:

- Luke 15
- Romans 5:8
- Acts 1:8
- Luke 15:24b

Memos of Mountaintop Moments

Chapter 29
SCALE THE WALL

With your help I can advance against a troop; with my God I can scale a wall. 2 Samuel 22:30

Sitting down with someone like Leta Mae brings a new and fresh perspective to life. You would think that someone who spent a period of her life eating nothing but potatoes and water, someone who lost her husband to cancer, or someone who has had her fair share of sorrows, would feel disappointed or depressed. Instead, she sees the eight decades of her life as filled with God moments, pivotal points, in which the faithfulness of her Savior was seen over and over again.

Yes, Leta Mae was chased by armies of fear, doubt, and insecurity. She faced walls that needed to be scaled. But God empowered her to scale the walls like David in Psalm 22:30. She did not go around the walls or stay stuck at their bases, but she moved closer to God, knowing that an upward-moving relationship with Christ was what she needed.

Leta's **higher ground** moments were many, but in this meeting, she shared three important ones. The first was on the steps of her dorm room in college. The second was in her Fresno home. The third was on her fireplace hearth. First let's look at some of her background story.

Leta Mae was born into a pastor's home in New Mexico. She was at the church just about every time the doors were opened. She gave her heart to the Lord at the age of five. When she turned six, her dad became the district superintendent, meaning he oversaw the pastors of the New Mexico District Nazarene churches. She remembered her dad walking around with a Bible and a hammer. He was intent on developing lives and constructing buildings. Another thing Leta Mae remembered is how some of the small churches and pastors struggled, both financially and emotionally. Those observations and perceptions would play into her thoughts significantly at a later time.

As a fourteen-year-old teenager, Leta Mae deepened her commitment to the Lord. She nailed down her faith as her own, and made a decision to continue to live for Jesus. She met Bert Rhodes in high school, and they fell in love. The problem was, he was called to be a pastor. Leta Mae knew that was not the path she wanted for her life, so they parted ways and went to separate colleges. Leta Mae missed Bert, even though she knew he wasn't the one for her. Upon returning to Pasadena College after Christmas of her sophomore year, she realized she was miserable without him.

She made the lonely climb up the stairs to her dorm room. The stairs became a place of **higher ground,** holy ground, if you will. She talked to the Lord about her resistance to being a pastor's wife. She gave God her dreams of having a home with a white picket fence someday. She let Him know that she was willing to suffer a life of martyrdom. She listed all the miserable things that she perceived would be part of her life, like having to move often, and laid them at Jesus' feet. God met her there, wrapped her in peace and love, and promised to be with her through it all.

Leta Mae laughed as she reflected on what an adventure her life had been since that day. She scaled the walls of her insecurities and doubts. She and Bert were married in December, 1950, and they began a venture together that never ceased to amaze and thrill them both. All these years later, Leta Mae can see how those things she was worried about back on those dorm steps either diminished in importance or never came to fruition.

Like her dad, Bert was motivated by transforming lives and constructing church buildings. Early in their marriage, Bert was helping his brother-in-law with a building project. He was finishing school, working on the church, and running a business delivering newspapers. During this busy season, Bert was called to the Pixley Nazarene Church. It was a small church in a small town, about a three-and-a-half-hour drive from where they were living. On Friday mornings, they would arise at the crack of dawn and drive to their place of ministry for the weekend. They would return on Sunday nights to go through the same weekly routine.

They were paid very little, and a baby was now in the mix. When Bert graduated and they were able to move to the little town, they were able to afford only potatoes for themselves and some powdered milk and oatmeal for their young child. It was at this time that Leta Mae decided she would get a teaching job to help with their income. She hadn't finished college, and she didn't have her credential. She confesses that she didn't know what she was doing and cried every day, but God helped her to get through it. The extra money helped with their needs.

After a few years in Pixley, they moved to Farmington, New Mexico. The church needed a parsonage, so Bert set out to help build one. In the meantime, their little family lived in the church's attic. The project was completed, and their nineteen months of ministry in this community came to an end. They were called back to California and pastored the Fresno First Nazarene Church for the next four to five years.

None of the things they had been through really bothered Leta Mae. She saw them as fun challenges. But when Bert was experiencing dark days, it was a different story. Being a pastor of a congregation is hard. People are not perfect. There can be criticism, decision making, and internal problems that get you down. Bert was having a difficult time maintaining his joy because of some of these issues. One night, while Bert was at a board meeting, Leta Mae determined that she was going to pray for him and for their situation. She knelt by her bedside and prayed a very short and simple prayer. She felt her own spirit lifted to **higher ground**. There was such sweet peace and hope, and she knew things were going to be alright.

Bert came home from his meeting and announced that he was ready to move on. They rejoiced and leaned into God for direction. Dedicated to finishing the current building project, they stayed two more years, but there was a sweet release of the problems to God. Eventually they moved to Bakersfield to pastor the Olive Knolls Church. It was the last time they would move to a new church or town. Bert and Leta Mae enjoyed a fruitful ministry at Olive Knolls. Of course, they were part of another building project, and their next twenty-five years were full of exploits that could be in a chapter of their own.

They now owned their own house, not with a picket fence, but definitely in a beautiful neighborhood. They also owned a cabin in the hills above Bakersfield. So many of the fears of her young life were dispelled and completely reversed. But Satan knew of her weakness and attempted to get a foothold. A pastor friend of theirs had passed away, and the wife was basically left destitute. Leta Mae began to fret about what would happen to her if Bert were to die.

Once again, her imagination went wild, spinning her into a lonely and scary time which she felt she could share with no one. She held onto her fears for quite a while, but knew she needed to commit them to the Lord. On a day when Bert was traveling out of town, she was determined to pray through her anxieties and doubts. She sat in the living room with her Bible, journals, and study material surrounding her. She sought and prayed throughout the day. Toward evening, a complete peace settled over her. She remembered the clock chiming 8:00 p.m., so she had literally been at it all day.

The joy that filled her was so exhilarating she did something she had never done before and hasn't done since. She jumped up on the fireplace hearth and danced unto the Lord. Once again, God came through and brought her to a place of **higher ground**, literally (I'm not sure how high her hearth was) and spiritually. She knew with a renewed reminder of God's faithfulness, that He would take care of her, no matter what.

In 1982, they were on a three-week sabbatical at their cabin. While Bert studied downstairs, Leta Mae spent time reading and studying upstairs. God gave her a sweet gift through her studies, a renewed commitment and love for her husband. It wasn't something she struggled with, but it was an overwhelming confirmation in her life to love him well, no matter what.

In 1985 Bert was diagnosed with cancer. His prognosis was grim, and they worked through the physical, spiritual and emotional pain together. Leta Mae had many opportunities to put into practice her love for him. In 1988, Bert succumbed to the disease, and went to be with Jesus. He lived well, and the memorial service was packed with hundreds of people who had been blessed by his life and ministry.

God is so amazing. He had already brought Leta Mae to a place of trust and comfort so many years before, that she would be taken care of. At Bert's passing, Leta Mae was burdened with hospital and doctor bills of more than $30,000. As she leaned on God's promise to be faithful to her, she worked with the insurance company, who was slow in getting all the bills paid and up-to-date. By the time all was said and done, it was a reasonable amount she was able to pay down over time.

Life didn't always go her way, but God gave her the strength and power through His Spirit to scale the walls of difficulty. We all have moments, pivotal points, where we must renew our faith and nail down our convictions in God. God has shown again and again that He wants to carry our burdens and lift us up.

SUMMING IT UP:

- At times we feel chased by armies of fear, doubt, and insecurity. We can face the walls that need to be scaled with God's power. An upward-moving relationship with Christ is what will lift us over those walls.
- When we surrender our dreams and fears to God, He saves us from our own perceived defeats.
- God saves us from periods of darkness and gives us light and hope in the middle of the problems.
- God meets us at the point of our fears, imagined or real, and lifts us up into a place of peace and joy.

☀ HIGHLIGHTS FROM GOD'S WORD:
- 2 Samuel 22:30
- 2 Samuel 22:20
- 2 Samuel 22:29
- 2 Samuel 22:34

Memos of Mountaintop Moments

Chapter 30
GOD GOES BEFORE YOU

The Lord himself goes before you and will be with you; he will never leave you nor forsake you. Do not be afraid; do not be discouraged. Deuteronomy 31:8

The hot temperature and arid climate contrasted with the cool air-conditioned interior of the pickup truck. The trees displayed their full green leaves as Mary, Paul, and Terry drove through the pistachio orchards. The stereo was playing familiar and sweet hymns, and Terry, Mary's elderly mom, sang and hummed along. She was content to be viewing the close-to-harvest nut clusters, God's handiwork through agriculture. When the song "Blessed Assurance" began to play, Terry sang along, not missing one word. She basked in God's presence, seeing the fruit of the trees, reflecting on the fruit of her life, and resting in the promise that "Jesus is mine." The memory was a precious one for Mary, and one that would help her through her mom's final days.

Mary enjoyed these special moments of connecting with her mom. In fact, having a close-knit family was part of the charmed life that Mary described as her growing-up years. Both her parents were teachers. There were five siblings close in age. They sat around the table for dinner each night, and never missed spending holidays together.

In September 2014, some of that charmed life began to unravel. Word came that her fifty-eight-year-old brother had been diagnosed with stage four pancreatic cancer. By the time it was detected, the cancer had already settled into his liver and lungs. He chose an aggressive and experimental chemo treatment, but between the second and third treatments he had a pulmonary embolism. He died on November 6, 2014, just a couple of months after the initial discovery.

Shortly after getting word of the diagnosis, each sibling and their parents had purchased plane tickets to visit him on November 12 at his home in Virginia. Though they did not see their brother before his passing, having the tickets scheduled a couple of months in advance was one of the ways that made the final days easier to handle. It was one less detail they had to worry about as they prepared to attend his memorial service. God had gone before them.

Mary sensed a recurring reminder from God throughout the next few years that He was going before them. The promise of Deuteronomy 31:8, "The Lord is the one who goes ahead of you; He will be with you. He will not fail you or forsake you. Do not fear or be dismayed," was being seen and felt each step of the way. Through the past trials and tragedies as well as the ones still to come, she could clearly see the hand of God paving the way and helping her through.

Still reeling from their brother's death, their family, who had no previous history of cancer, would soon be shocked by the discovery of two more cancer cases. Mary's sister was diagnosed and treated for thyroid cancer. Doctors also discovered prostate cancer in her second brother. Fortunately, these two siblings were able to receive timely treatments, and they have both passed their five-year cancer-free markers with flying colors.

Understandably, Mary began to feel every tweak and pain, imagining the worst each time. She began experiencing stress and anxiety. Her doctor suggested counseling, but also did a thorough physical exam. The exam revealed that she had a nodule on her thyroid. Before she could make an appointment at Sansum clinic, God again paved the way.

At just the right time, Mary happened to run into a friend who had just been through a similar thyroid issue. She gushed about her endocrinologist as being the kindest, most thorough doctor she had ever known. Mary got an appointment to see her friend's doctor. The doctor did a biopsy and decided to remove half of the thyroid.

God was good and His timing perfect. When the surgery was scheduled, Mary was granted the earliest time slot available that day. This helped alleviate the worry and stress of waiting all day for her procedure. According to the doctor, the surgery went well. He had made the decision to remove the entire thyroid instead of half. Before Mary and her husband, Paul, had driven too far down the road to head back home post-surgery, they got a call from the surgeon. The results were already back showing that it had been cancerous. He knew that his instincts to take the entire thyroid had been correct.

Not long after her recovery, the focus shifted from the siblings to their parents. Mary's dad started to decline in health. Though he remained sharp mentally, the stress of losing a son and dealing with other family issues was overwhelming. When her mom called to say he was in the hospital, the family rallied around. Their dad was going to need to transition to an assisted living facility since their mom could no longer provide the care he would need.

The hospital representative's first communication about moving their dad had felt stiff and rote, and the first places they checked out were cold and uninviting. Mary decided to try a different approach when she called back the representative. She expressed her appreciation for her and offered to pray for her, acknowledging the stress she must face each day. As they continued to talk, the representative softened. She was able to recommend an additional possible placement, much closer to where her mom lived. At this point, it was no surprise. God was going ahead of them. This latest assisted living facility felt right, and it had three beds open. Her dad settled into his new place, but his health continued to decline. Within a couple of weeks, he made his final transfer to his heavenly home.

The family was now seeing a waning in their mom's mental state. For those who have been through the journey with an aging parent, especially one with some form of dementia or Alzheimer's, the stress of watching your parent go through this is painful. As you observe them change, the repetition of questions and conversation can get exhausting. Their perception of what is real feels bazaar. Their behaviors and dialog can be frustrating and strange.

Mary made the three-and-a-half-hour journey to visit her mom almost every week. Her mom was having hallucinations of visitors coming into the house at night and of her deceased son conducting a choir in the backyard. Mary's sister moved from Oklahoma so that someone would be with her on a consistent basis. Mary continued her trips to give the local family a break.

One night Mary and her sister had just settled in for the night after a tough encounter with their mom that had involved a call to 911. At 2:00 AM the doorbell rang. The same policemen who had been at the house earlier were at the door with Mary's mom. She had been found down the street, in her pajamas, with her purse on her shoulder, kneeling in front of a neighbor's house.

With this increase in her dysfunction, the family got busy checking out referrals to some Alzheimer's facilities. The third place they visited, Blossom Grove, specialized in Alzheimer and dementia care. It was smaller and more intimate than some of the others they had checked out. The staff immediately began showing tender care.

God had provided the family with His peace that they were making the right decision. One of her mom's nurses, Aurora, had previously worked in their family doctor's office. She was familiar with the family and with Terry. She was always warm, friendly, and welcoming. This was yet another example of God's grace going before them. Here was a familiar face—someone who had history with the family— making the transition a little easier.

Truly, there was nothing easy about the situation. Many days, their mom would let them know she would not be talking to any of them. Other times she could be wooed with a jar of her favorite chocolates or a cheeseburger and shake. The kids all tried to visit as much as possible, but it was like talking to a stranger. They would come in to find her things packed, and she would declare that she was moving back to the blue house, wherever that might have been.

Mary was grateful that she had walked with a friend recently who had been on this path. It had helped prepare her heart for what she was now facing. Though difficult and trying at times, she knew how important it was to honor her parents, who had provided and nurtured them for so many years. The family also realized they were not alone in this journey as they watched other families with loved ones at Blossom Grove.

When the Covid-19 pandemic hit, things changed, especially in elderly care facilities. No one was allowed to go inside to visit her. The staff would wheel Mary's mom to the window to see her children, but there was no physical touch or inside visitations. Whether it was the natural course of life events, or whether the isolation catapulted her health issues, we will probably never know.

On April 20, Mary was at home in Bakersfield, walking with a friend. Her brother called to say the hospice nurse thought that their mom had less than two weeks to live. Something inside Mary told her she needed to go right then. Mary got in the car and listened to worship music as she drove south. She checked into a hotel around 8:00 p.m., then immediately went to the assisted living facility. They put Mary through a Covid protocol, allowing her to go into her mom's room.

Mary was greeted by a nurse, Melissa, who remembered her dad as her school counselor and her mom as her English teacher. She told Mary how much she loved talking to her mom. Mary had regularly treated Melissa and other staff with pistachios. It was her way to say thank you and show sensitivity to the care they were giving to her mom and all the patients each day.

When Mary went into her mom's room, her mom was not conscious. Donning a purple nightgown, her favorite color, Terry looked like a shell of who she had been. Mary noted that her hair had been brushed back, she was very pale, her mouth was agape, and she looked small and frail.

It was now about 8:25 p.m. Mary held her mom's hand, and reminded her how much they all loved her, naming all the kids and grandkids. She used her phone to play "Blessed Assurance," remembering the precious moment months earlier when her mom had been able to sing along.

At around 8:42 p.m., Mary breathed a prayer, "Lord, can you just come get her?" Immediately, Mary felt a physical whooshing, much like the air had been sucked out of the room, followed by a peaceful presence. Mary was certain that Jesus came at that moment and ushered Terry to **higher ground**. Her mom's face changed to a look of peace, and Mary knew she was gone.

Mary grabbed the nurse, Melissa, who came in disbelief because it had happened so quickly, yet confirmed that her mom had passed. Mary didn't feel sad. She was just joyful knowing that her mom was no longer suffering, but was enjoying the presence of Jesus and her loved ones who had gone before her.

Again, due to the Covid limitations, the funeral was attended by siblings and spouses and a couple of nieces, a limited total of ten people. A deacon from the church, who was a good family friend, officiated the service. The scripture reading, a talk by her brother, and a song by one of the nieces was live-streamed for the rest of the family members.

Terry never again got to drive through the pistachio groves, but she was loved and cared for in the best possible way at Blossom Grove. As she was escorted by Jesus from death to eternal life, she was no doubt singing with confidence, "Blessed assurance, Jesus is mine!" Her foretaste of glory was now a divine reality.

Summing it Up:

- We can reflect at any point in our lives on the fruitfulness and faithfulness of God's presence in our lives.
- God goes before us and paves the way for what is to come long before we experience the need for His grace and mercy.
- Though it can be trying at times, it is important for us to honor our parents until the end.
- We can have assurance through believing in Jesus and His word that our eternal life is secure.

Highlights from God's Word:

- John 15:16; Galatians 5:22-23
- Deuteronomy 31:8
- Ephesians 6:2-3
- John 5:24

Memos of Mountaintop Moments

Made in the USA
Columbia, SC
16 May 2022